SOCIO-ECONOMIC DISPARITIES AMONG SOCIAL GROUPS IN INDIA

SOCIO-ECONOMIC DISPARITIES AMONG SOCIAL GROUPS IN INDIA

Edited by
K. Ramesh

SERIALS PUBLICATIONS
NEW DELHI

First Published-2010

ISBN: 978-81-8387-382-6

Published by

SERIALS PUBLICATIONS
4830/24, Prahlad Street, Ansari Road
Darya Ganj, New Delhi-110002 (India)
Phone : 23245225 Fax : 91-11-23272135
E-mail: serials@sify.com

CONTENTS

Preface vii

1. Spatial and Inter-temporal Disparities in Sex Ratio among Social Groups in India 1
   K. Ramesh
2. Social Disparities in Access to Health Care in India 17
   Ti. M. Swaaminathan
3. An Analysis of Differentials in Neonatal and Infant Mortality Rates in India and Tamilnadu 25
   D.B. Usha Rani & R. Sumathi
4. Rural–Urban Disparity in Education 36
   Leela Bhaskar
5. Social Disparity in Educational Attainment: A Micro Level Study 45
   N. Palaniraj
6. Educational Attainment and Welfare Interventions for the Under-privileged in Pondicherry 56
   D. Uma
7. Obstacles to School Life Expectancy 64
   J. Maheswari
8. Gender Disparity in Education-Extent and Factors – India 73
   S. Raja Rajan
9. Caste and Labour Market Discrimination in Tamil Nadu 85
   V. Sivasankar
10. Disparities among Social Groups in Employment and Wage Rates in India 94
    R. M. Jagannathan
11. Socio-economic Study of Child Labour in Ottapidaram Taluk Tuticorin District 102
    D. Amutha & J. Ellora
12. Social Transformation: An Ethnographic Exploration of Malayalis, Yelagiri Hills, Tamil Nadu 111
    L. Kathiresan
13. Micro Finance: SHG – Bank Linkage Programme 121
    C. Dhandapani
14. Divergence of Land Reforms in India 127
    P. Anbalagan

PREFACE

India is a large federal nation and it is a fact that there are widespread disparities in the levels of economic and of social development between the different regions. It is well known that interregional economic disparities increase, at least in the initial stages of national economic development. As a result, governments everywhere including India used to initiate deliberate policy measures to reduce these disparities. However, with the re-arrival of the market mechanism in the liberalised economic scenario the world over now, there is a tendency to withdraw such measures under the implicit assumption that the 'invisible hand' will deliver the goods.

India has also witnessed a sea change in its economic policy, of late. There was serious concern then at the fact that some Indian states with large populations and vast natural and mineral resources were pockets of poverty. In such a scenario, widespread inter-state disparities in levels of economic and social development can have serious economic, social and even political consequences, this being particularly so if these have persisted over long periods of time.

Economic development and social development are mutually reinforcing and so also disparities. Socially excluded are economically marginalized and *vice versa*. The gains of economic development accrue disproportionately to the socially developed groups. On the other hand, socially backward may gain only marginally from economic development which may not be sufficient for them to improve their social skills to enable them to earn more. This vicious circle transcends from generation to generation. There exist several dimensions of economic and social disparities of development in the country.

Thus, in a plural society like India, with people of different castes and religions, it is equally important to focus on 'horizontal inequalities' i.e. disparities between certain identifiable groups such as the scheduled castes (SC) and scheduled tribes (ST), who comprise a quarter of India's total population. There are separate provisions for their welfare in the 'Constitution of India', which form the basis of targeted development policies by the State to raise the socioeconomic status of these groups in absolute terms as well as relative to the rest of society.

The 11th Five Year Plan document has reiterated that, "Our ultimate objective is to achieve broad based improvement in the living standards of all our people. We also need to ensure that growth is widely spread so that its benefits, in terms of income and employment, are adequately shared by the poor and weaker sections of our society, especially the SCs and the STs, and others. For this to happen, the growth must be inclusive in the broadest sense. It must occur not just in our major cities but also in our villages and small towns. It must generate sufficient volumes of high quality employment to provide the means for uplift of large numbers of our population from the low income low quality occupations in which too many of them have been traditionally locked. The Eleventh Plan addresses itself to the challenge of making growth both faster and more inclusive". While efforts are being taken to reduce the social and economic inequalities that remain among different social groups, the process of globalisation and privatisation calls for putting a safety net to protect the vulnerable groups from being worsening further. However, the efforts being taken by the government is only a piece meal attempt, since there is a formidable imbalance even in the availability of quality time series data on various socio-economic aspects of the under-privileged groups. Paucity of data has also culminated in the paucity of literature about the socio-economic disparities among the social groups in India. This is a potential danger in the sense that without the necessary data and the accompanying literature, no worthwhile effort can be made to improve the conditions of the vulnerable groups in a permanent manner.

This calls for a concerted effort to fill this void and thus an attempt is made here by collecting articles from various authors on varied themes and topics, focussing on the socio-economic disparities among the social groups in India. I thank all the contributors for their effort and enthusiastic participation in this endeavour, which has made this work possible. I also thank my wife **Devika Rani** MCA, sons **Gautham** and **Rahul** and other family members for their support and encouragement. I thankfully acknowledge the unstinting support extended by the staff members of Serials Publications which has made this book to come out at a quick time.

Chennai **K. RAMESH**

01.01.2010

LIST OF CONTRIBUTORS

K. Ramesh, Reader, PG and Research Department of Economics, Presidency College, Chennai-600 005.

Ti. M. Swaaminathan, Assistant Professor, PG and Research Department of Commerce, Pachaiyappa's College for Men, Kanchipuram-631 501.

D.B. Usha Rani, Reader and **R. Sumathi**, Assistant Professor, Department of Economics, Ethiraj College for Women, Ethiraj Salai, Chennai-600 008.

Leela Bhaskar, Reader, Department of Economics, Ethiraj College for Women, Ethiraj Salai, Chennai-600 008.

N. Palaniraj, Associate Professor, Department of Economics, Pachaiyappa's College for Men, Kanchipuram-631 501.

D. Uma, Associate Professor, Department of Economics, Ethiraj College for Women, Ethiraj Salai, Chennai-600 008.

J. Maheswari, Assistant Professor, Dept Of Economics, Quaid-E-Millath Govt College For Women, Anna Salai, Chennai-2

S. Rajarajan, Reader in Economics, PG & Research Deparment of Economics, Government Arts College (Autonomous), Kumbakonam-1

V. Sivasankar, Assistant Professor in Economics, Muthurangam Government Arts College, Vellore-632 002.

R.M. Jagannathan, Associate Professor, Department of Economics, Pachaiyappa's College for Men, Kanchipuram-631 501.

D. Amutha, Assistant Professor, Department of Economics, St. Mary's College, Tuticorin and **J. Ellora**, Associate Professor, Department of Commerce, St. Mary's College, Tuticorin.

L. Kathiresan, Research Scholar, Centre ot Social Medicine & Community Health, School of Social Sciences, Jawaharlal Nehru University, New Delhi-110 067.

C. Dhandapani, Reader in Economics, Muthurangam Government Arts College, Vellore-632 002.

P. Anbalagan, Reader, PG and Research Department of Economics, Presidency College, Chennai-600 005.

1

SPATIAL AND INTER-TEMPORAL DISPARITIES IN SEX RATIO AMONG SOCIAL GROUPS IN INDIA

K. RAMESH

INTRODUCTION

In a developing society and economy, sex ratio is an important indicator of social and political equity among the genders. In the process of development, however, sex ratio changes in favour of males, which is particularly true in the case of East Asian countries. In India too, worsening of sex ratio has taken place over the years which has been captured by the successive Censuses. In a vast country like India, there bound to be spatial variations among different social groups in the sex ratio. This paper tries to bring out the existing disparities in sex ratio among different states of India as well as different segments of the society with the help of 1991 and 2001 Census data.

SEX RATIO OF TOTAL POPULATION

Table 1 presents the sex ratio of total population in 17 major states of India, separately for rural and urban areas. It also provides the deviation in the sex ratio of each state from the national average and also the inter-census growth rate. It can be noted from the table that the sex ratio of total rural population at the all - India level in 1991 stood at 939, which means there were 939 females for every 1000 males, which had increased marginally to 946 in 2001 and thereby registering a growth rate of 0.75 per cent between the two periods. At the state level, Kerala had the highest rural sex ratio of 1037, while Haryana had the lowest sex ratio of 863. Among the 17 major states, in three states, viz., Haryana, Punjab and Uttar Pradesh (UP), the rural sex ratio was less than the 900 mark, which indicates a spatial trend. In all the southern states, the rural sex ratio was higher than the level of 970, though Kerala had a remarkable figure of 1037 in 1991.

In 2001, the rural sex ratio had declined from the level of 1991 in three states viz., Gujarat, Himachal Pradesh (HP) and Maharashtra, though in the latter two states it was higher than the national average, while in Gujarat

Table 1
Area-wise Sex Ratio of Total Population in Major States of India

States	Rural					Urban				
	1991	Deviation*	2001	Deviation*	GR (%)	1991	Deviation*	2001	Deviation*	GR (%)
Andhra Pradesh	977	38	983	37	0.61	958	64	965	65	0.73
Assam	934	-5	944	-2	1.07	837	-57	872	-28	4.18
Bihar	921	-18	933	-13	1.30	844	-50	868	-32	2.84
Gujarat	950	11	945	-1	-0.53	908	14	880	-20	-3.08
Haryana	863	-76	866	-80	0.35	866	-28	847	-53	-2.19
Himachal Pradesh	992	53	989	43	-0.30	920	26	795	-105	-13.59
Jammu & Kashmir	N.A.	N.A.	917	-29	N.A.	N.A.	N.A.	819	-81	N.A.
Karnataka	973	34	977	31	0.41	930	36	942	42	1.29
Kerala	1037	98	1059	113	2.12	1034	140	1058	158	2.32
Madhya Pradesh	943	4	947	11	0.42	893	-1	905	5	1.34
Maharashtra	972	33	960	14	-1.23	875	-19	873	-27	-0.23
Orissa	988	49	987	41	-0.10	866	-28	895	-5	3.35
Punjab	888	-51	890	-56	0.23	868	-26	849	-51	-2.19
Rajasthan	919	-20	930	-16	1.20	879	-15	890	-10	1.25
Tamil Nadu	981	42	992	46	1.12	960	66	982	82	2.29
Uttar Pradesh	884	-55	936	-10	5.88	860	-34	864	-36	0.47
West Bengal	940	1	950	4	1.06	858	-36	893	-7	4.08
All-India	939	Nil	946	Nil	0.75	894	Nil	900	Nil	0.67

Note: * indicates deviation from the national average. GR – Inter-Census growth rate. Census was not conducted in J&K in 1991.

Source: Calculated from Census of India, 1991 and 2001, Govt. of India, New Delhi.

it was less by one. In 2001 also, there was no change in the best and worst performed states in rural sex ratio, though the gap had widened between the two. Once again, the four southern states, viz., Andhra Pradesh (AP), Karnataka, Kerala and Tamil Nadu (TN) performed better as their rural sex ratios had gone up in 2001 from that of 1991. In Kerala especially, the sex ratio had increased from 1037 to 1059, registering a growth rate of 2.12 per cent. Growth rate-wise, it was the highest in UP with 5.88 per cent as the rural sex ratio had increased from 884 to 936, while it was the lowest in Maharashtra with a negative growth rate of 1.23 per cent as the rural sex ratio had declined from 972 to 960.

The urban sex ratio at the all-India level and also at the individual state level was markedly less compared to that of rural sex ratio in both time periods, which implies the spatial disparity in sex ratio. At the all-India level, urban sex ratio had increased from 894 in 1991 to 900 in 2001, though in both time periods, as mentioned above, the figures were less than the rural sex ratio. This indicates that in urban India, there were only 894 females for every 1000 males, which increased just to 900 in 2001. Table also suggests that except in six states (Andhra, Gujarat, Himachal Pradesh (HP), Karnataka, Kerala and TN), the urban sex ratio was less than 900 in 1991. In Kerala too, the urban sex ratio was less than its rural sex ratio. Chart 1 portrays the area-wise all-India sex ratio of the total population.

Chart 1: Area-wise Sex Ratio of Total Population, 1991 and 2001, All-India

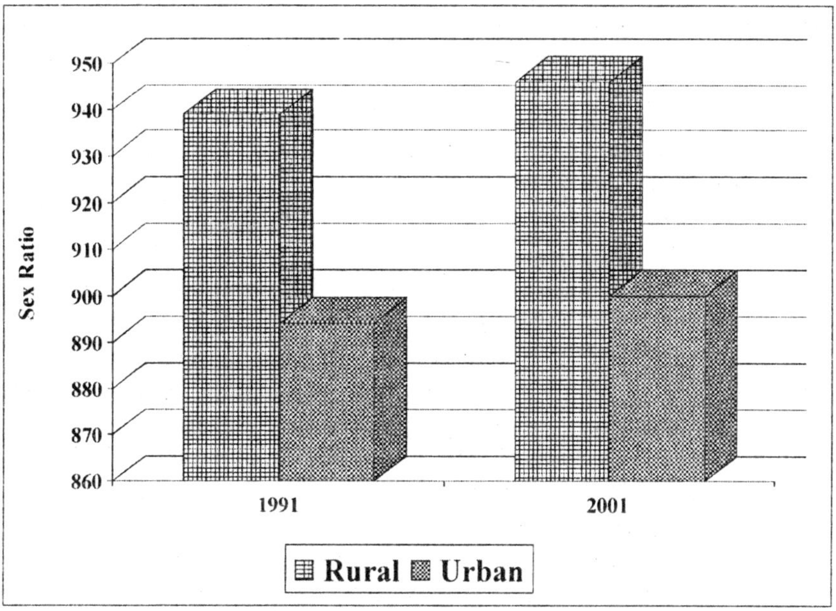

Source: Based on Table 1.

In 2001, sex ratio in the urban areas had declined in five states (Gujarat, Haryana, HP, Maharashtra and Punjab) from that of 1991. In other states, though the urban sex ratio had gone up in 2001, the rate of increase was quite less and thus the national average had increased only by 6, from 894 to 900. This indicates that in total population, rural sex ratio had differed considerably from the urban sex ratio, where the sex ratio of the latter was less in all the states including Kerala.

SEX RATIO OF NON-SC & ST POPULATION

The Non-SC & ST population forms the major part of the total population of the country and thus, the trend in the former will influence that of the latter. The area-wise sex ratio of the non-SC & ST population in 1991 and 2001 in the major states of India is presented in Table 2.

It can be noted from the table that the all-India rural sex ratio of the non-SC & ST population in 1991 was 937, which increased to 942 in 2001 and in both time periods, the sex ratio was marginally less than that of the total population for the corresponding periods. The table indicates that there was not much difference in the rural sex ratio of total population and that of non-SC & ST population among the states in 1991, except in two states, viz., Madhya Pradesh (MP) and Punjab. In the former, the rural sex ratio of total population was higher than that of non-SC & ST population, while in the latter, it was the other way round. In this case also, the worst and best performed states were the same, viz., Haryana and Kerala respectively.

In 2001, the rural non-SC & ST sex ratio had gone up in all but four states, viz., HP, Maharashtra, Orissa and Punjab. The inter-Census growth rate implies that in Gujarat, the rural sex ratio had increased by the highest percentage of 7.42 followed by UP with 6.44 per cent. The comparison of the rural sex ratio growth rates of total population and that of non-SC & ST population suggests that the latter (0.53 per cent) was less that of the former (0.75 per cent). This shows that there was less number of females among the non-SC & ST segment of the population than among the total population at the all-India level.

The urban sex ratio of the non-SC & ST population indicates that at the all-India level, it was less than that of the urban sex ratio of total population in both Censuses. It had increased nevertheless from 892 to 896 and thus, among the non-SC & ST population, there were less than 900 females for every 1000 males. In 1991, the urban sex ratio was more than 900-mark in only five states, viz., Andhra, Gujarat, Karnataka, Kerala and TN. In 2001, the urban sex ratio had decreased in five states, viz., Gujarat, Haryana, HP, Maharashtra and Punjab. The decline in the urban sex ratio of HP was the highest as it had declined from 827 to 767 between the two Censuses with a negative growth rate of 7.26 per cent, while its rural sex ratio had witnessed only a marginal fall by 0.30 per cent. This

Table 2
Area-wise Sex Ratio of Non-SC & ST Population in Major States of India

States	Rural					Urban				
	1991	Deviation*	2001	Deviation*	GR (%)	1991	Deviation*	2001	Deviation*	GR (%)
Andhra Pradesh	981	44	985	43	0.41	957	65	962	66	0.52
Assam	928	-9	940	-2	1.29	831	-61	864	-32	3.97
Bihar	916	-21	929	-13	1.42	839	-53	863	-33	2.86
Gujarat	944	7	1014	72	7.42	906	14	876	-20	-3.31
Haryana	865	-72	865	-77	0.00	869	-23	844	-52	-2.88
Himachal Pradesh	996	59	993	51	-0.30	827	-65	767	-129	-7.26
Jammu & Kashmir	N.A.	N.A.	917	-25	N.A.	N.A.	N.A.	817	-79	N.A.
Karnataka	975	38	977	35	0.21	927	35	938	42	1.19
Kerala	1039	102	1061	119	2.12	1034	142	1058	162	2.32
Madhya Pradesh	927	-10	931	-11	0.43	891	-1	902	6	1.23
Maharashtra	974	37	957	15	-1.75	868	-24	865	-31	-0.35
Orissa	983	46	979	37	-0.41	849	-43	882	-14	3.89
Punjab	895	-42	888	-54	-0.78	866	-26	839	-57	-3.12
Rajasthan	920	-17	930	-12	1.09	880	-12	888	-8	0.91
Tamil Nadu	982	45	990	48	0.81	958	66	979	83	2.19
Uttar Pradesh	885	-52	942	0	6.44	861	-31	863	-33	0.23
West Bengal	938	1	945	3	0.75	852	-40	887	-9	4.11
All-India	937	Nil	942	Nil	0.53	892	Nil	896	Nil	0.45

Note: * indicates deviation from the national average. GR – Inter-Census growth rate.
Source: Calculated from Census of India, 1991 and 2001, Govt. of India, New Delhi.

was similar to its decline in the overall sex ratio, particularly again among the urban population, which indicates that urban areas of HP are heading towards a huge social crisis. The all-India growth rate of the urban sex ratio was only 0.45 per cent, which is again less than that of the total population. Thus, the sex ratios of the non-SC & ST population among both rural and urban areas in both time periods were less than that of the total population in India.

SEX RATIO OF SC & ST POPULATION

The sex ratio of the SC & ST population in both rural and urban areas in 1991 and 2001 is presented in Table 3. The table indicates that the rural sex ratio of the SC & ST population in 1991 stood at 943 which had increased to 954 in 2001, registering a remarkable growth rate of 1.17 per cent. Thus, the rural sex ratio of this segment of the population was higher than not only that of non-SC & ST population, but also that of total population. The sex ratio was less than 900-mark in only three states, viz., Haryana, Punjab and UP, while in other states it was higher than 900 and in Kerala, it stood at 1025. In the case of SC & ST population too, the three states, Haryana, Punjab and UP had the lowest figures *vis-a-vis* the national average, as it had happened in the case of total population and non-SC & ST population.

In 2001, the rural sex ratio among the SC & ST population had increased in all but one state, viz., Gujarat. The sex ratio in Gujarat had declined quite sharply from 963 to 809, by a whopping –15.99 per cent. However, as the sex ratio had gone up in all other states, the all-India sex ratio had increased to 954 in the rural areas. In urban areas, the sex ratio of the SC & ST population had moved up from 908 to 927, achieving an inter-Census growth rate of 2.09 per cent. Thus, in the urban sex ratio too, the figure among the SC & ST population was higher than that of non-SC & ST population and also that of total population in both time periods, though it should also be mentioned that as it had occurred in other cases, the urban sex ratio was considerably less than that of the rural sex ratio. The higher sex ratio among the SC & ST population in both rural and urban areas in both time periods might be due to a higher family size compared to that among the non-SC & ST population. Chart 2 presents the comparative view of the area-wise sex ratio of both non-SC & ST and SC & ST population at the all-India level.

SEX RATIO OF THE 0-6 POPULATION

The sex ratio of the population in the age group of 0-6 is an important indicator of the social development which is taking place in the country. The area-wise and state-wise sex ratio of the 0-6 population during 1991

Table 3
Area-wise Sex Ratio of SC & ST Population in Major States of India

States	*Rural*					*Urban*				
	1991	*Deviation**	*2001*	*Deviation**	*GR (%)*	*1991*	*Deviation**	*2001*	*Deviation**	*GR (%)*
Andhra Pradesh	967	24	977	23	1.03	965	57	984	57	1.97
Assam	955	12	961	7	0.63	876	-32	928	1	5.94
Bihar	937	-6	949	-5	1.28	875	-33	903	-24	3.20
Gujarat	963	20	809	-145	-15.99	919	11	916	-11	-0.33
Haryana	857	-86	870	-84	1.52	848	-60	867	-60	2.24
Himachal Pradesh	981	38	981	27	0.00	1264	356	930	3	-26.42
Jammu & Kashmir	N.A.	N.A.	918	-36	N.A.	N.A.	N.A.	842	-85	N.A.
Karnataka	967	24	977	23	1.03	944	36	961	34	1.80
Kerala	1025	82	1044	90	1.85	1030	122	1053	126	2.23
Madhya Pradesh	965	22	970	16	0.52	901	-7	918	-9	1.89
Maharashtra	967	24	969	15	0.21	921	13	940	13	2.06
Orissa	996	53	997	43	0.10	932	24	947	20	1.61
Punjab	873	-70	894	-60	2.41	874	-34	887	-40	1.49
Rajasthan	917	-26	931	-23	1.53	875	-33	897	-30	2.51
Tamil Nadu	978	35	996	42	1.84	977	69	1001	74	2.46
Uttar Pradesh	880	-63	907	-47	3.07	854	-54	869	-58	1.76
West Bengal	945	2	959	5	1.48	893	-15	929	2	4.03
All-India	943	Nil	954	Nil	1.17	908	Nil	927	Nil	2.09

Note: * indicates deviation from the national average. GR – Inter-Census growth rate.
Source: Calculated from Census of India, 1991 and 2001, Govt. of India, New Delhi.

Chart 2: Area and Group-wise Sex Ratio, 1991 and 2001, All-India

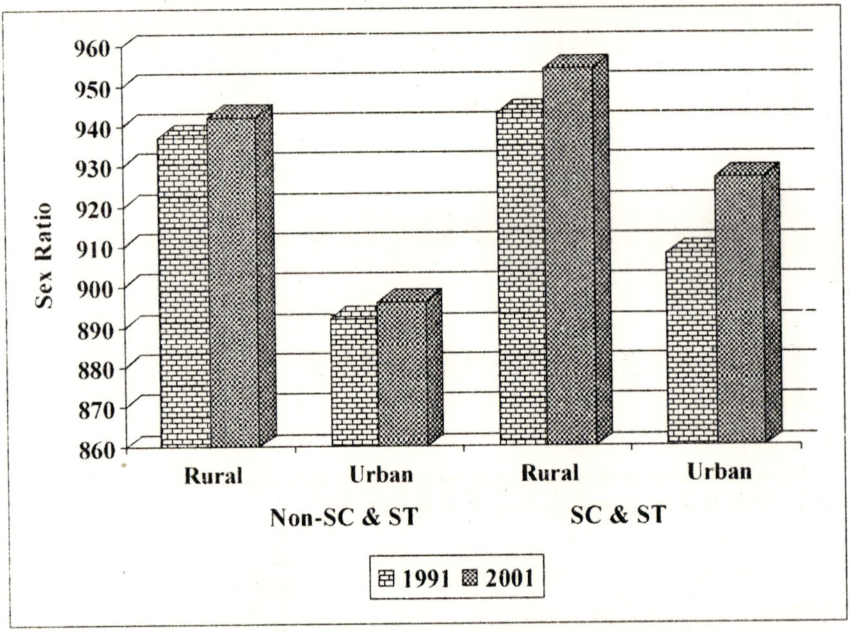

Source: Based on Tables 2 and 3.

and 2001 is presented in Table 4. It can be inferred from the table that the rural sex ratio of the 0-6 population at the all-India level is 1991 which stood at 947 was higher than any other segment in that time period. State-wise, there is a change in the worst and best performed states in the sex ratio of this segment. Andhra Pradesh had the highest sex ratio of 979 while, HP had the worst figure at 820 and thus, no state had a sex ratio of more than 1000 including Kerala. This clearly marks a departure from the sex ratio of other segments. Three states viz., Haryana, HP and Punjab had the less than 900-mark figures.Another departure from the earlier trends was that the rural 0-6 sex ratio had declined from 947 in 1991 to 934 in 2001 with a negative growth rate of 1.37 per cent. This had occurred as in 14 out of 16 states (Census was not conducted in J&K in 1991), the rural 0-6 sex ratio had declined in 2001, the states with a positive growth rate being HP and Kerala. The sex ratio in Punjab had gone below the 800-mark in 2001, registering a negative growth rate of 9.1 per cent. This undeniably indicates the fact that the child sex ratio in the rural areas of the major states had come down which signifies an alarming trend. The sex ratio in HP had improved though it still remained less than the national average. Moreover, in Punjab and Haryana, the deviation was more than 100 in the negative side.

In the urban areas, the sex ratio of 0-6 population which was 935 in 1991 had fallen drastically to 906 in 2001, with a growth rate of –3.1 per

Table 4
Area-wise Sex Ratio of 0-6 Population in Major States of India

States	*Rural*					*Urban*				
	1991	*Deviation**	*2001*	*Deviation**	*GR (%)*	*1991*	*Deviation**	*2001*	*Deviation**	*GR (%)*
Andhra Pradesh	979	32	963	29	-1.63	961	26	956	50	-0.52
Assam	977	30	967	33	-1.02	961	26	941	35	-2.08
Bihar	961	14	950	16	-1.14	951	16	926	20	-2.63
Gujarat	936	-11	906	-28	-3.21	909	-26	837	-69	-7.92
Haryana	877	-70	822	-112	-6.27	886	-49	807	-99	-8.92
Himachal Pradesh	820	-127	899	-35	9.63	906	-29	853	-53	-5.85
Jammu & Kashmir	N.A.	N.A.	957	23	N.A.	N.A.	N.A.	869	-37	N.A.
Karnataka	963	16	949	15	-1.45	951	16	940	34	-1.16
Kerala	958	11	961	27	0.31	957	22	958	52	0.10
Madhya Pradesh	956	9	930	-4	-2.72	936	1	899	-7	-3.95
Maharashtra	952	5	916	-18	-3.78	935	0	908	2	-2.89
Orissa	969	22	955	21	-1.44	948	13	933	27	-1.58
Punjab	879	-68	799	-135	-9.10	867	-68	796	-110	-8.19
Rajasthan	919	-28	914	-20	-0.54	909	-26	887	-19	-2.42
Tamil Nadu	945	-2	933	-1	-1.27	955	20	955	49	0.00
Uttar Pradesh	928	-19	921	-13	-0.75	929	-6	889	-17	-4.31
West Bengal	969	22	963	29	-0.62	955	20	948	42	-0.73
All-India	947	Nil	934	Nil	-1.37	935	Nil	906	Nil	-3.10

Note: * indicates deviation from the national average. GR – Inter-Census growth rate.
Source: Calculated from Census of India, 1991 and 2001, Govt. of India, New Delhi.

cent between the two Censuses. Thus, in this case also, the urban sex ratio was less than that of rural areas. State-wise, Andhra Pradesh and Assam had the highest sex ratio at 961, while it was the lowest in Punjab at 867. Thus, in Punjab, both the rural and urban sex ratios were less than 900 and the only other state which had this dubious distinction was Haryana. Punjab and Haryana, both being agriculture dominated states (at least until 2001), had preferred more male children.

In 2001, the urban 0-6 sex ratio had declined in all states with the exception of Kerala, in which it had increased very negligibly by 0.1 per cent, while there was no change in the sex ratio of TN. The number of states which had less than 900-mark had gone up from just two in 1991 to eight in 2001. Thus, son preference had become quite widespread in 2001. Moreover, the fall that had taken place in the urban sex ratio was quite significant as in three states the decline was around 8 per cent, while in another seven states it was more than 2 per cent.

SEX RATIO OF 7+ POPULATION

The sex ratio of the 7+ population among the major states in both rural and urban areas is analysed in this section with the help of the data presented in Table 5. The rural sex ratio of the 7+ population at the all-India level in 1991 was 937 which had increased to 948 in 2001 with a growth rate of 1.17 per cent. The rural sex ratio was less than 900 in only three states viz., Haryana, Punjab and UP, in which Haryana had the lowest figure at 860, while Kerala had the highest sex ratio at 1050. In 1991, HP too had a sex ratio of more than 1000 in its rural areas.

In 2001, the all-India rural sex ratio of the 7+ population had increased to 948, since in all but two states (HP and Maharashtra), the sex ratio had gone up. Thus, only one state (Haryana) had less than 900-mark sex ratio, while in four states (HP, Kerala, MP and TN) the rural 7+ sex ratio was 1000 or more.

In the urban areas, the sex ratio of the 7+ population in 1991 was 887 which had moved up to 900 in 2001 with a growth rate of 1.47 per cent between the two periods. Thus, unlike the child sex ratio, the 7+ sex ratio had moved up in both areas between 1991 and 2001, while the urban sex ratio of the 7+ population was typically less than that of the rural areas in 1991 as well as in 2001. Between 1991 and 2001, the urban sex ratio had declined in Gujarat, Haryana, HP and Punjab, in which the decline in HP was the worst, as it had come down from 922 in 1991 to 789 in 2001. Moreover, only in Kerala, the sex ratio was more than 1000 in both 1991 and 2001. Chart 3 presents the segment-wise sex ratio at the all-India level.

CHANGES IN SEX RATIO AMONG THE STATES

The sex ratios of the states in both rural and urban areas have undergone changes between 1991 and 2001. Moreover, there are also spatial variations

Table 5
Area-wise Sex Ratio of 7+ Population in Major States of India

States	*Rural*					*Urban*				
	1991	*Deviation**	*2001*	*Deviation**	*GR (%)*	*1991*	*Deviation**	*2001*	*Deviation**	*GR (%)*
Andhra Pradesh	977	40	986	38	0.92	958	71	966	66	0.84
Assam	923	-14	940	-8	1.84	818	-69	864	-36	5.62
Bihar	911	-26	929	-19	1.98	823	-64	858	-42	4.25
Gujarat	952	15	953	5	0.11	907	20	887	-13	-2.21
Haryana	860	-77	875	-73	1.74	862	-25	853	-47	-1.04
Himachal Pradesh	1026	89	1004	56	-2.14	922	35	789	-111	-14.43
Jammu & Kashmir	N.A.	N.A.	910	-38	N.A.	N.A.	N.A.	813	-87	N.A.
Karnataka	975	38	982	34	0.72	926	39	942	42	1.73
Kerala	1050	113	1073	125	2.19	1045	158	1071	171	2.49
Madhya Pradesh	940	3	1009	61	7.34	884	-3	931	31	5.32
Maharashtra	977	40	968	20	-0.92	864	-23	868	-32	0.46
Orissa	992	55	992	44	0.00	853	-34	890	-10	4.34
Punjab	889	-48	905	-43	1.80	868	-19	857	-43	-1.27
Rajasthan	919	-18	934	-14	1.63	873	-14	890	-10	1.95
Tamil Nadu	987	50	1000	52	1.32	961	74	985	85	2.50
Uttar Pradesh	872	-65	938	-10	7.57	846	-41	861	-39	1.77
West Bengal	934	-3	948	0	1.50	845	-42	886	-14	4.85
All-India	937	Nil	948	Nil	1.17	887	Nil	900	Nil	1.47

Note: * indicates deviation from the national average. GR – Inter-Census growth rate.
Source: Calculated from Census of India, 1991 and 2001, Govt. of India, New Delhi.

Chart 3: Segment-wise Sex Ratio, 1991 and 2001, All-India

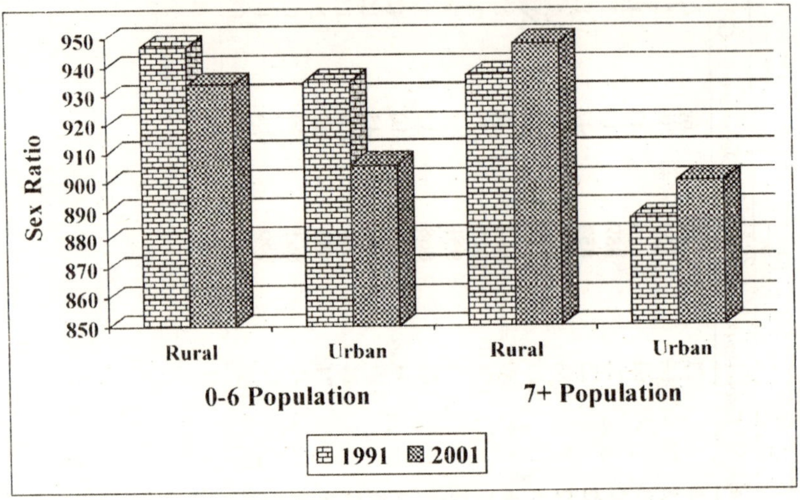

Source: Based on Tables 4 and 5.

in the sex ratios of the states. This section analyses the changes in the position of states' sex ratios *vis-a-vis* the national average, area and Census-wise. Table 6 presents the changes in the sex ratio in the total population.

It can be observed from the table that in six states, viz., Haryana, UP, Punjab, Rajasthan, Bihar and Assam the rural sex ratio of total population was less than the national average, while in other states, viz., West Bengal

Table 6
Total Population Sex Ratio: Area-wise Position of States

Below National Average	*Total Population*	*Above National Average*
Haryana, UP, Punjab, Rajasthan, Bihar, Assam	*1991 Rural*	WB, MP, Gujarat, Maharashtra, Karnataka, AP, TN, Orissa, HP, Kerala
Assam, Bihar, WB, UP, Haryana, Orissa, Punjab, Maharashtra, Rajasthan, MP	*1991 Urban*	Gujarat, HP, Karnataka, AP, TN, Kerala
Haryana, Punjab, J&K, Rajasthan, Bihar, UP, Assam, Gujarat	*2001 Rural*	MP, WB, Maharashtra, Karnataka, AP, Orissa, HP, TN, Kerala
HP, J&K, Haryana, Punjab, UP, Bihar, Assam, Maharashtra, Gujarat, Rajasthan, WB, Orissa	*2001 Urban*	MP, Karnataka, AP, TN, Kerala

Source: Based on Table 1.

(WB), MP, Gujarat, Maharashtra, Karnataka, AP, TN, Orissa, HP and Kerala it was higher than the national average. However, in the case of urban areas, the sex ratio was less than the national average in 10 states, viz., Assam, Bihar, WB, UP, Haryana, Orissa, Punjab, Maharashtra, Rajasthan and MP, while it was higher in only six states, Gujarat, HP, Karnataka, AP, TN and Kerala. Thus, more number of states had a below-than national average sex ratio in the urban areas than in the rural areas in 1991.

In 2001, the number of states which had below-than national average sex ratio in the rural areas had increased to eight (Haryana, Punjab, J&K, Rajasthan, Bihar, UP, Assam and Gujarat), in which J&K and Gujarat joining the list in 2001 and thus the other states, viz., MP, WB, Maharashtra, Karnataka, AP, Orissa, HP, TN and Kerala had a above national average sex ratio. Among the urban areas, 12 states (HP, J&K, Haryana, Punjab, UP, Bihar, Assam, Maharashtra, Gujarat, Rajasthan, WB and Orissa) had a sex ratio which was less than the national average and thus only five states had a higher than national average sex ratio. This suggests that between 1991 and 2001, the number of states having less sex ratio than the national average had increased in both rural and urban areas, implying the fact that sex ratio had worsened among the total population in 2001.

The changing positions of the states in the non-SC & ST sex ratio are presented in Table 7. In 1991, among the rural areas, seven states had a less sex ratio (Haryana, UP, Punjab, Bihar, Rajasthan, MP and Assam),

Table 7
Non-SC&ST Population Sex Ratio: Area-wise Position of States

Non-SC&ST Population		
Below National Average		*Above National Average*
	1991 Rural	
Haryana, UP, Punjab, Bihar, Rajasthan, MP, Assam		WB, Gujarat, Maharashtra, Karnataka, AP, TN, Orissa, HP, Kerala
	1991 Urban	
HP, Assam, Bihar, Orissa, WB, UP, Punjab, Maharashtra, Haryana, Rajasthan, MP		Gujarat, Karnataka, AP, TN, Kerala
	2001 Rural	
Haryana, Punjab, J&K, Bihar, Rajasthan, MP, Assam		WB, Maharashtra, Karnataka, Orissa, AP, TN, HP, Gujarat, Kerala
	2001 Urban	
HP, J&K, Punjab, Haryana, Bihar, UP, Assam, Maharashtra, Gujarat, Orissa, WB, Rajasthan		MP, Karnataka, AP, TN, Kerala

Source: Based on Table 2.

MP joining the list which was not there under total population. In the case of urban areas also, HP comes under the list of 'below national average' along with 10 other states, all of which belonging to the northern belt of the country.

In 2001, among the rural areas Haryana, Punjab, J&K, Bihar, Rajasthan, MP and Assam had below national average sex ratio, which suggests that UP had moved out of this list compared to 1991, while J&K entering into this category. However, in the urban areas, the number of states which had below national average sex ratio was 12, viz., HP, J&K, Punjab, Haryana, Bihar, UP, Assam, Maharashtra, Gujarat, Orissa, WB and Rajasthan, while only MP, Karnataka, AP, TN and Kerala had above average sex ratio in 2001. This again suggests that the number of states having less than average sex ratio was higher in the urban areas than in the rural areas and in both areas, the number had gone up in 2001 from that of 1991.

Table 8 provides the details regarding the changing positions of the states in the SC & ST sex ratio. It can be noted from the table that the same trend of more states with less than average sex ratio in the urban areas and in 2001 is repeated in the case of SC & ST sex ratio also. Moreover, it also implies that the states like Haryana, Punjab, UP, Rajasthan and Bihar were quite notorious for their very poor sex ratio in all segments in both time periods. States like AP, Karnataka, TN and Kerala had performed better in all segments in both Censuses, while WB, HP, MP, Maharashtra and Assam had fallen in between and in the case of Gujarat, its sex ratio had worsened especially in 2001.

Table 8
SC&ST Population Sex Ratio: Area-wise Position of States

SC&ST Population		
	1991 Rural	
Below National Average		*Above National Average*
Haryana, Punjab, UP, Rajasthan, Bihar		WB, Assam, Gujarat, MP, AP, Karnataka, Maharashtra, TN, HP, Orissa, Kerala
	1991 Urban	
Haryana, UP, Punjab, Bihar, Rajasthan, Assam, WB, MP		Gujarat, Maharashtra, Orissa, Karnataka, AP, TN, Kerala, HP
	2001 Rural	
Gujarat, Haryana, Punjab, UP, J&K, Rajasthan, Bihar		WB, Assam, Maharashtra, MP, AP, Karnataka, HP, TN, Orissa, Kerala
	2001 Urban	
J&K, Haryana, UP, Punjab, Rajasthan, Bihar, Gujarat, MP		Assam, WB, HP, Maharashtra, Orissa, Karnataka, AP, TN, Kerala

Source: Based on Table 3.

The changing positions of the states in the child sex ratio are presented in Table 9 which indicates that the number of states coming under the less than average category was higher in both rural and urban areas and in both 1991 and 2001 than other segments of the population.

Table 9
Sex Ratio of 0-6 Population: Area-wise Position of States

Below National Average	*0-6 Population*	*Above National Average*
	1991 Rural	
HP, Haryana, Punjab, Rajasthan, UP, Gujarat, TN		Maharashtra, MP, Kerala, Bihar, Karnataka, Orissa, WB, Assam, AP
	1991 Urban	
Punjab, Haryana, HP, Gujarat, Rajasthan, UP		MP, Orissa, Bihar, Karnataka, TN, WB, Kerala, AP, Assam
	2001 Rural	
Punjab, Haryana, HP, Gujarat, Rajasthan, Maharashtra, UP, MP, TN		Karnataka, Bihar, Orissa, J&K, Kerala, AP, WB, Assam
	2001 Urban	
Punjab, Haryana, Gujarat, HP, J&K, Rajasthan, UP, MP		Maharashtra, Bihar, Orissa, Karnataka, Assam, WB, TN, AP, Kerala

Source: Based on Table 4.

Table implies that states like TN, MP, Gujarat and MP also come under the less than average sex ratio is an important deviation from the normal trend, though TN had a higher than average sex ratio in the 2001 Census in its urban areas.

The positions of the states in the sex ratio of their 7+ population in both rural and urban areas are shown in Table 10.

It can observed from the table that Haryana, UP, Punjab, Bihar, Rajasthan, Assam and WB had a sex ratio of below national average in 1991 in their rural areas, while the other states, viz., MP, Gujarat, Karnataka, AP, Maharashtra, TN, Orissa, HP and Kerala had above national average sex ratio. In the case of urban areas, typically, the number of states which had had below national average sex ratio was more than that of the rural areas. Assam, Bihar, WB, UP, Orissa, Haryana, Maharashtra, Punjab, Rajasthan and MP were those states which had a less than national average sex ratio, while Gujarat, HP, Karnataka, AP, TN and Kerala had above national average sex ratio. As far as the 2001 rural sex ratio was concerned, there was no change in the number of states with below national average figures, though there were some changes in the states *per se*. However, in the urban areas in 2001, except MP, Karnataka, AP, TN and Kerala, all other states had below national average sex ratio.

Table 10
Sex Ratio of 7+ Population: Area-wise Position of States

Below National Average	*7+ Population*	*Above National Average*
Haryana, UP, Punjab, Bihar, Rajasthan, Assam, WB	*1991 Rural*	MP, Gujarat, Karnataka, AP, Maharashtra, TN, Orissa, HP, Kerala
Assam, Bihar, WB, UP, Orissa, Haryana, Maharashtra, Punjab, Rajasthan, MP	*1991 Urban*	Gujarat, HP, Karnataka, AP, TN, Kerala
Haryana, Punjab, J&K, Bihar, Rajasthan, UP, Assam	*2001 Rural*	Gujarat, Maharashtra, Karnataka, AP, Orissa, TN, HP, MP, Kerala
HP, J&K, Haryana, Punjab, Bihar, UP, Assam, Maharashtra, WB, Gujarat, Orissa, Rajasthan	*2001 Urban*	MP, Karnataka, AP, TN, Kerala

Source: Based on Table 5.

CONCLUSION

This analysis about the spatial and inter-temporal trends in the sex ratio of different segments of population indicates that Punjab, Haryana, UP, Bihar and Rajasthan had very low sex ratio in both rural and urban areas in 1991 which had only worsened in 2001. States like AP, Karnataka, TN and Kerala had better sex ratios during 1991 which had increased in 2001. However, among all states, rural sex ratio was higher than the urban sex ratio, while in many states, sex ratio in general had gone up in 2001. But this general trend did not hold good in the case of child sex ratio, where it had fallen between 1991 and 2001 in both rural and urban areas and in no state, it was higher than 1000 including Kerala. Finally, sex ratio among the SC & ST population was higher than their Non-SC & ST counterparts in both areas and in both Censuses, which might have caused by the larger family size of the former.

REFERENCES

Census of India, 1991, Govt. of India, New Delhi.

Census of India, 2001, Govt. of India, New Delhi.

2

SOCIAL DISPARITIES IN ACCESS TO HEALTH CARE IN INDIA

TI. M. SWAAMINATHAN

INTRODUCTION

The National Health Policy (NHP), 2002 has set out the basic objective of achieving good health amongst all population of the country. The National Common Minimum Programme (NCMP) of the present Government has also placed emphasis on raising public health investment with focus on primary health care and increased investment in programmes to improve the reproductive and child health care. It envisages an increase in public spending on health to 2-3 per cent of GDP by increased contributions from the Central and State Governments. Towards this end the Government has launched a National Rural Health Mission (NRHM).

The NRHM be implemented throughout the country with special focus on 18 States with weak public health indicators and/or weak infrastructure; to improve the availability of and access to quality health care in general and to reproductive and child health care and to build synergy between health and determinants of good health like nutrition, sanitation, hygiene and safe drinking water. Accordingly, the targets are to reduce the Maternal Mortality Rate (MMR) to 100 per 100,000 live births by 2012; the Total Fertility Rate (TFR) to be reduced to 2.1 by 2012; and the Infant Mortality Rate (IMR) to be reduced to 30 per 1000 live births by 2012. These targets are prominently placed in achieving millennium development Goals (MDGs).

SOCIAL GROUPS

Caste and religion is intertwined with every aspect of life in India. The Hinduism is the largest religion, which is described as majority and followed by the Muslims, Christians and others including Sikhs, Buddhists and Jains, which are described as minorities. The Hindu Religion has further divided into different caste groups broadly termed as the Scheduled Castes, (SCs), the Scheduled Tribes (STs), the Other Backward Classes

(OBCs) and Others. According to 2001 Census, the Hindus constitute about 80.5% and within it the SCs representing 16.2 per cent, the STs account for 8.2 per cent of the country's total population. In the absence of specific Census data, it is not possible to quote the exact figure for the OBCs, but NFHS and NSS estimates roughly about 32-37%. The minorities, who constitute 19.5%, represent Muslims about 13.4 per cent, Christians 2.3 per cent, Sikhs 1.8 per cent, Buddhists 0.8 per cent and Jains 0.4 and others 0.7 per cent to total population in India.

The Constitution of India guarantees social, economic and political provisions for protection and promotion of interest of the SCs/STs, the OBCs and the Minorities. In order to bring them at par with the rest of society by adopting the approach of social justice to ensure equal rights, access to public services and resources to enable them to develop their potential and capacities as agents of social change, through the process of planned development.

The discussion here is focuses on equity perspective of the present health status and patterns of health care access and utilization by different social groups viz. SCs/STs and OBCs others and the religious minorities both in absolute term and relative terms. The National Family Health Survey NFHS-III (2004-05) provides recent information on aspects of health status, access to health care, and utilization of health service by different sections of population in India.

EQUITY IN HEALTH

Generally the assessment health conditions of population, it is often restrict to a few measurable aspects, such as mortality, morbidity, and nutritional status. The health status of individuals affects their capabilities both in gaining access to socio-economic opportunities and therein community at large. Other things being equal, a better health status enhances the capabilities and productive skills of individuals. Differentials in the health status of individuals in a population, in tandem with differentials in other basic endowments, will have a bearing on their pattern of access and utilization to health care services. Following sections describe the attainment of these indicators and difference between caste and religious groups in India.

MORTALITY

Mortality is an important indicator and reflects a country's level of socio-economic development and quality of life of population. It indicates that rate of death occurred in given period of time for 1000 population. The NFHS gives major three mortality rate related to children namely, Infant Mortality Rate (IMR), Child Mortality Rate (CMR) and Under-five Mortality Rate (U5MR) reflects the probability of dying in early childhood.

Infant Mortality Rate is the proportion of newborn dying before completion of the first year of age. According to the NFHS-III, the infant mortality rate for Hindus 77 per thousand much higher than Christians (49 per 1000) and Muslims (59 per 1000), but close to the average for India (73 per thousand) as a whole. Similarly, in case of child mortality and under-five mortality rates are again higher for the Hindus followed by Muslims and Christians. About 32 per thousand children born in Hindu have probability of dying between 1 and 5 years of age, this is 25 per thousand for Muslims and 19 per thousand for Christians. In case of under-five mortality rate, again the level is much higher for the Hindus as about 107 per thousand live birth dies before completing five years of age. The level was much lower for the Christians 68 and as 83 for Muslims well below for the national average, 101 per thousand live births.

Mortality Indicators for Castes and Religious Groups - India, 2006-07

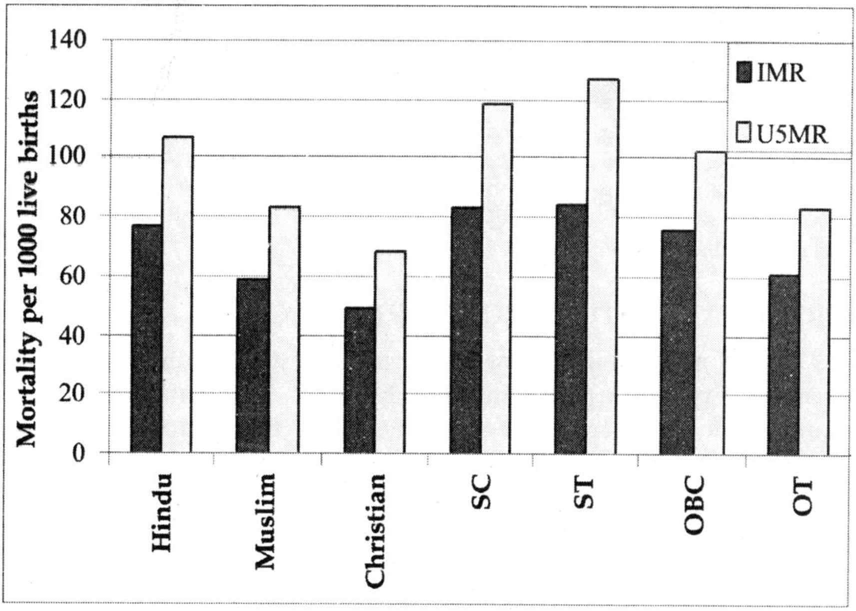

MORBIDITY

Morbidity is another important indicator of health status of population. Given the limitation of the data, we discuss prevalence of Acute Respiratory Infection (ARI), and diarrhoea. ARI primarily pneumonia, is a major cause of illness among infants and children and diarrhoea is a major killer disease for children under age five worldwide. ARI/pneumonia and dehydration is fairly common and, if no early diagnosis treatment is provided, could lead to death (IIPS 2000). Acute respiratory infection and diarrhoea are generally prevail among all the religious groups at 20% rate except the diarrhoea is relatively low among the Christians 16% as compared with Hindus and Muslims about 20%.

Morbidity Indicators for Castes and Religious Groups - India, 2006-07

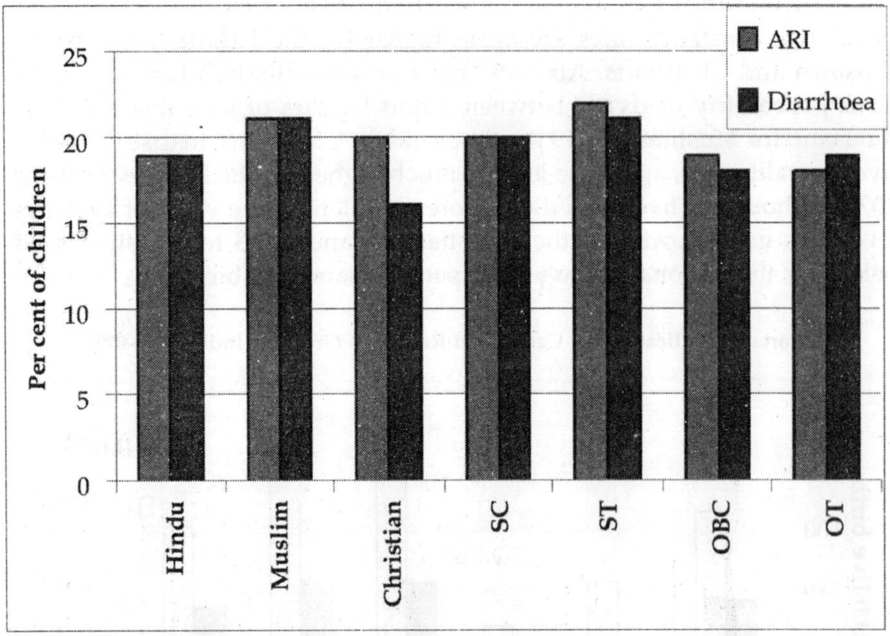

NUTRITIONAL STATUS AMONG CHILDREN

Under nutrition is a major factor responsible for the high morbidity and high mortality among the Indian children. The anthropometric measurements in the two NFHS surveys show that nearly half of the children have weights too low for their age compared to international standards and are classified as undernourished. Further the survey reveals that undernourished prevails generally among all religious groups expect among Christians. It is high among children belongings to SCs and STs as about 55% of suffer as undernourished. The lowest level of under nutrition is seen among Christian (30%) from religious groups and among other caste (40%) among caste groups. Similarly among women the nutritional status seem to persist in same patterns (see the figure below).

Prevalence of Under Nutrition among Castes and Religious Groups All-India, 2006–07

Access to Health Care

Access to health care generally assessed in terms of indicators such as vaccination of children; vitamin A supplementation; antenatal check-up; TT injection and IF supplements; institutional delivery; and medical assistance at birth. Following section looks at these indicators and its variation among caste and religious groups.

Vaccination & Vitamin 'A' Supplementation

Children are future assets and get special care in a society. As part of this special care Universal Immunization Programme (UIP) was introduced in the mid 80s in all districts of the country with the objective of covering at least 85 per cent of all infants against preventable diseases till 1990. For a child, the recommended set of immunizations includes three doses each of DPT antigen (diphtheria, pertussis, tetanus) and polio vaccine, one dose of BCG (against tuberculosis), and one dose of measles vaccine, before the completion of one year of age. The NFHS has obtained data on these for the children of age 12-23 months at survey from the women interviewed in the survey shows indicator of percent of children that received all the recommended doses (BCG, measles, three doses each of DPT and polio) as well as the percent of children that received none of these.

The coverage is far from being universal, only about 42 percent of children received all the recommended doses in India. There is difference between three major religious groups, Christians and Hindus have, over 60% and 42%, whereas and Muslims with (32%) that less than national average of 42% full immunisation. Among caste groups the rate of immunisation (full vaccination) was higher for others about 47% and lower for STs about 27% of children and 30% for SCs.

In case of vitamin A supplementation, NFHS-III gives information on children of age 12-35 months who received at least one dose is quite dismal about only 30 per cent children received. Children belongings to Christians received vitamin A are 33% and among Hindus are 30% and for Muslims about only 24% are well below the national average. Among social groups again the SCs/STs gets low than the other caste.

ANTE NATAL CARE – ANTENATAL CHECK-UP & TT INJECTION

Antenatal care refers to pregnancy related health care and importance to receive adequate doses to tetanus toxoid (TT) vaccine and other health check-up. The NFHS-3 estimates that during the late 1998-99 ante-natal check-up was conducted by qualified professionals in case of 65 per cent of births. Christians generally does and received both the check-up and TT vaccine (85%) as compare to other religious groups (65-70%). Among the caste groups taking TT and antenatal care was fairly widespread results only marginal variation.

DELIVERY CARE: INSTITUTIONAL DELIVERY& MEDICAL ASSISTANCE AT BIRTH

In India, a majority of deliveries, especially in rural areas, continue to take place at home irrespective of caste and religion. But this is relatively low among Christians. The NFHS-3 estimates of percentage of deliveries at home are about 45% for Christians and about 66-67 for Hindus and Muslims. Among caste groups, the percentage is very high for SCs/STs about 70-80 and low for others. In case of professional assistance at delivery, about 34 percent of deliveries were assisted by a professional, that is, a doctor or trained midwife/health workers. The SCs/STs are less in receiving medical assistance during delivery as compare to others.

FINANCING HEALTH CARE: THE INDIVIDUAL AND THE STATE

When we look at the profile of diseases we can see that rural–urban differential in the proportion of hospitalization within each ailment is negligible, except for the heart diseases, where the proportion of hospitalization cases in the urban areas was almost double that in the rural areas. The average medical expenditure on health for both hospitalization and non-hospitalization cases in rural areas is lower than in urban areas. However, household income lost per treated person is much higher in the rural areas (Rs 135) than urban (Rs 96) for non-hospitalization cases. In either scenario, private players play a dominant role.

There are demonstrated differences between the payment patterns of the rich and the poor in both inpatient and outpatient care. Those from poorer sections depend more on income and less on savings (as they are likely to have minimal savings). Similarly, in the event of a negative health occurrence, the poorest sections are most propendent to sell their assets. It is also not surprising that friends and relatives are significant contributors to health care costs. What is however surprising is that although clearly identifiable differences exist between the financing sources of the poorest and richest segments, the differences are not dramatic. What is also interesting is that the differences in hospitalization cost between public and private facilities have a magnitude of 2. In other words, the private sector does not appear to be charging much more than public facilities. While significant user charges are being paid by all economic segments for availing of health care services, the question remains as to who will pay for the expansion and rationalization of health care facilities to augment physical, technical as well as human resource infrastructure to cater better to the needs of the economically challenged sections of the society. Clearly it is not the user but the state or the central government budget that must bear the load of this expense.

CONCLUSION

While summing up, the foregoing analysis shows that, there are inequality among social groups in health status and access to health care and this difference is relatively smaller among religious groups as compare between caste groups. Even though a well-structured public health care system exists, the infrastructure as well as the staff that are required to provide the health care services is inadequate from many different perspectives. Many rural residents are not able to obtain treatment for basic ailments either due to the non-presence of health care services in the vicinity, or due to lack of funds to access the same. Even for basic health care services such as reproductive and child health, we find that significant proportions continue to remain untreated. Immunization, ante-natal care, deliveries in the presence of professionally trained personnel, and so on all show large unmet needs figures. The private sector is filling in the unmet need to an extent and this role is rapidly expanding. Today private sector health care provision in rural areas is *greater* than that by the public sector. But despite the presence of a large, dynamic, and what appears to be a well spread out private health care provision network, access issues remain important because in remote and far flung habitations, the private sector does not have the incentive to set up shop and in the absence of adequate penetration by public sector health centres, these areas remain unserved. But, there is little consensus on the possible answer. Under the new scenario, regulatory mechanisms and the role of new information technologies have come under the scanner as possible solution baskets in providing accessible and effective quality healthcare to the vast Indian rural populations.

A question which is begging an answer is what should be the role of the current public health care system. Though public–private partnerships are growing, there are still financial as well as logistical constraints to starting large scale ventures under such arrangements. Thus, ineffective and inadequate public service has paved way for the growth of the private sector health care in the country. The private sector is not only filling up the gaps left by the public sector but is also emerging as the key player in terms of service provision. But in terms of quality of service both the public and the private sector have failed. The two most important issues which emerge with regard to rural health infrastructure in the country are lack of access for many and poor quality of service.

REFERENCE

Banerjee A., Esther C. Duflo, and Angus Deaton (2004), 'Healthcare Delivery in Rural Rajasthan', *Economic and Political Weekly*, 39(9), pp. 944-949, Mumbai.

Chaudhury N., J. Hammer, M. Knemer, K. Muralidharan, and F.H. Rogers (2006), 'Missing in Action: Teacher and Health Worker Absence in Developng Countries', Volume 20, November 1, *Journal of Economic Perspectives*, Pittsburg.

International Institute for Population Sciences and ORC Macro (2000), India: National Family Health Survey (NFHS-2), 1998-99.

MHFW (2005), *Rural Health Care System in India*, Ministry of Health and Family Welfare, Government of India, New Delhi.

NSSO (2004), *Morbidity,Health Care and the Condition of the Aged,* NSSO 60th Round, Report No. 507(60/25.01/1), National Sample Survey Organisation, Ministry of Statistics and Programme Implementation, New Delhi.

RBI (2004), *State Finances – Study of Budgets,* Reserve Bank of India, Mumbai.

World Bank (2006) - *India: Inclusive Growth & Service Delivery: Building on India's Success,* World Bank, Washington D.C.

3

AN ANALYSIS OF DIFFERENTIALS IN NEONATAL AND INFANT MORTALITY RATES IN INDIA AND TAMILNADU

D.B. USHA RANI & R. SUMATHI

India faces the problem of population explosion, poverty, illiteracy, unemployment and poor health conditions. Socio-economic and socio-cultural factors that exist in an economy lead to poverty. Poverty affects the most vulnerable, the children. The healthy growth of children is fundamental for future economic progress. A country depends on its healthy citizens for increased productivity and growth. Children form the special risk group because of the risk involved in their development and survival.

The Indicators that reflect child survival and mortality are,

	Indicators	*Period*
1)	Neonatal Mortality Rate	(0-27 days)
2)	Post Neonatal Mortality Rate	(28 days - 11 months)
3)	Early Neonatal Mortality Rate	(0-7 days)
4)	Late Neonatal Mortality Rate	(7 days - 28 days)
5)	Peri-Natal Mortality Rate	(28 weeks of gestation + 0-7 days)
6)	Stillbirth Rate	(28 weeks of gestation)
7)	Infant Mortality Rate	(0-1 year)
8)	Under Five Mortality Rate	(0-5 years)

NEONATAL MORTALITY RATE

It is the death occurring in the first four weeks of life after birth. It includes Peri-Natal mortality, which is the death occurring in the first seven days of life and foetal deaths. One in three children under the age of five dies in neonatal period. Therefore, to reduce under-five mortality rate, it is necessary to reduce neonatal deaths.

Mortality rates of the infants in the first month of life have remained relatively constant at around 30/1000 live births, which results in four million deaths per year. 60 to 80 per cent of all newborn deaths is due to low birth weight at a weight less than 2500g or 5 pounds, 8 ounces – at birth.[1]

India with Highest Number of Newborn Deaths

More than two-thirds of all newborn deaths occur in just 10 countries of the world, which are 2.7 million deaths out of 4 million each year. India ranks first among the countries with the highest number of newborn deaths, followed by China.

Table 1 highlights the highest ranking of countries with newborn deaths. India and China tops the list because of the population size and have a very high percentage. In some countries such as Afghanistan, Congo and Tanzania, due to poor economic and health conditions, the numbers of newborn deaths is very high. More than 60 per cent of maternal deaths occur in these countries.

Table 1
Countries with Highest Number of Newborn Deaths

Country	*Number of Newborn Deaths*	*Ranking for Number of Newborn Deaths*
India	1,098,000	1
China	416,000	2
Pakistan	298,000	3
Nigeria	247,000	4
Bangladesh	153,000	5
Ethiopia	147,000	6
Democratic Republic of Congo	116,000	7
Indonesia	82,000	8
Afghanistan	63,000	9
United Republic of Tanzania	62,000	10

Source: Lawn, J.; Cousens, S. and Zupan, J. (2005), "4 Million Neonatal Deaths, When? Where? Why?", *Lancet*, Vol. 365, pp. 891-900.

Neonatal Mortality in India and Tamil Nadu

India faces the challenge of child survival and the associated health problems. Nearly 26 million infants are born each year, of which 1.2 million die before completion of the first 4 weeks of life and 1.7 million die before reaching the first birthday. Forty seven per cent of infant deaths occur in the first week of life.[2] India has taken note of the Millennium Development Goals and it has included in its Agenda a number of targets. The Health Targets[3] are,

1) Reduction of Infant Mortality Rate to 45/1000 live births by 2007 and to 28/1000 live births by 2012.

2) Millennium Development Goals indicate that Under-Five Mortality Rate must be reduced from 125 deaths per 1000 live births in 1988-92 to 41 in 2015.

Table 2 provides information on NMR in India and Tamil Nadu from 1971 to 2003 based on residence. In 1971, NMR for rural and urban India was 80.6 and 45.4 respectively. It was 53.3 and 51.4 for Tamil Nadu. The rural-urban differential at All India level was 35.2, which was only 1.9 for Tamil Nadu. However, from 1973, the rural-urban differential for Tamil Nadu was comparatively high. This was due to under reporting of neonatal deaths in rural Tamil Nadu during that period. In rural areas majority of deliveries were home deliveries.

In 1985, the rural-urban differential was 33.3 and 31.9 for India and Tamil Nadu respectively. Even though neonatal mortality rate of urban

Table 2

Neonatal Mortality Rate in India and Tamil Nadu Based on Residence from 1971-2003

Year	*India*			*Tamil Nadu*		
	Rural	*Urban*	*Rural-Urban Differential*	*Rural*	*Urban*	*Rural-Urban Differential*
1971	80.6	45.4	35.2	53.3	51.4	1.9
1972	76.6	44.9	31.7	56.6	55.1	1.5
1973	72.1	47.5	24.6	52.1	35.2	16.9
1974	75.7	41.0	34.7	50.7	44.1	6.6
1975	84.3	46.2	38.1	56.0	40.2	15.8
1976	83.0	49.0	34.0	51.5	40.9	10.6
1977	88.0	42.0	46.0	88.0	50.0	38.0
1978	85.2	38.0	47.2	79.5	34.5	45.0
1979	77.7	42.4	35.3	77.3	37.2	40.1
1980	75.5	39.1	36.4	67.6	41.4	26.2
1981	75.6	38.5	37.1	71.2	38.1	33.1
1982	72.9	38.8	34.1	66.1	31.1	35.0
1983	73.6	39.3	34.3	67.9	37.8	30.1
1984	72.2	39.7	32.5	66.4	35.5	30.9
1985	66.6	33.3	33.3	66.9	35.0	31.9
1986	65.5	36.2	29.3	67.0	37.1	29.9
1987	63.6	33.3	30.3	55.3	32.3	23.0
1988	62.0	34.6	27.4	62.7	30.7	32.0
1989	62.1	31.4	30.7	60.4	29.9	30.5
1990	57.4	30.9	26.5	52.3	27.1	25.2
1991	55.4	32.2	23.2	49.3	29.6	19.7
1992	53.6	33.0	20.6	49.2	30.2	19.0
1993	52.3	28.4	23.9	54.9	27.9	27.0
1994	52.0	32.6	19.4	45.7	33.9	11.8
1995	52.3	29.2	23.1	47.0	25.0	22.0
1996	50.0	28.0	22.0	45.0	28.0	17.0
1997	50.5	26.2	24.3	42.8	29.0	13.8
1998	49.0	27.0	22.0	39.0	27.0	12.0
1999	49.0	28.0	21.0	39.0	29.0	10.0
2000	49.0	27.0	22.0	41.0	24.0	17.0
2001	44.0	25.0	19.0	35.0	25.0	10.0
2002	44.0	24.0	20.0	36.0	17.0	19.0
2003	41.0	22.0	19.0	33.0	21.0	12.0

Source: Computed from SRS Bulletins, Registrar General, New Delhi, India.

areas of both India and Tamil Nadu is declining, the high prevalence of NMR in rural areas off-set the fall in overall NMR. In 2003, the rural NMR of India was 41.0, which was twice the rate of urban NMR of 22.0. Because of high NMR in rural areas, the decline in NMR is slowing down.

INFANT MORTALITY RATE IN INDIA AND TAMIL NADU

According to the Sample Registration System, April 2006, the five States with low IMR were Kerala (12), Maharashtra (36), West Bengal (40), Tamil Nadu (41) and Punjab (45). Five States with high IMR were Madhya Pradesh (79), Orissa (77), Uttar Pradesh (72), Rajasthan (67) and Chattishgarh (66). Tamil Nadu ranks fourth among bigger States in India in 2004 with 41/ 1000 live births In 2004, Tamil Nadu (Rural) (45) has been placed fourth after Kerala (13), West Bengal (42), Maharashtra (42). Whereas in urban areas Tamil Nadu (35) ranks sixth after Kerala (9), Maharashtra (27), Delhi (30), West Bengal (32) and Jharkhand (34). (SRS,2006).

Even though the achievements of Tamil Nadu are commendable, it is more than three times higher than Kerala's and there are differentials in Rural and Urban. The trends indicate that there is considerable slowing down in the falling rate.

Table 3 depicts infant mortality rate in India and Tamil Nadu based on residence. In 1971 IMR in rural India and rural Tamil Nadu were 138 and 127 respectively, TN's IMR was below National average. In 1981, rural-urban differential for India was 57 compared to 49 for Tamil Nadu. From 1981 onwards, urban IMR for India fell down to 62 showing improved infant health care in urban areas of the country and the State. In 1991, IMR for rural areas of India touched 87 while for Tamil Nadu it reached 66. In 2004, IMR for rural and urban India were 64 and 40 respectively, while it was 45 and 35 for urban and rural Tamil Nadu showing a major breakthrough in infant care because of Universal Immunisation Programme and Pulse Polio Programme.

Causes for Infant Mortality in Rural and Urban Tamil Nadu

According to the Director of Census Operation, Tamil Nadu,[4] the causes of death of infants in rural areas are respiratory infection of the newborn, prematurity, congenital malfunction, diarrhoea of the newborn and birth injury. These causes account for 80 per cent of death in rural areas of Tamil Nadu. In urban areas, slow foetal growth, malnutrition, prematurity, birth trauma, birth asphyxia, congenital disorders, infectious and parasitic diseases, viral diseases are the major causes of death of infants.

According to WHO (1998), as IMR falls to 50/1000 live births, congenital disorders begin to contribute significantly to infant and child mortality. At this stage genetic and birth defects are placed among the three leading causes of infant mortality. India's urban IMR has touched the mark of 50/1000 live births in 1990 and has been hovering around 40

Table 3
Infant Mortality Rate in India and Tamil Nadu Based on Residence, 1971-2003

Year	*India*			*Tamil Nadu*		
	Rural	*Urban*	*Rural-Urban Differential*	*Rural*	*Urban*	*Rural-Urban Differential*
1971	138	82	56	127	77	50
1972	150	85	65	133	85	48
1973	143	89	54	122	67	55
1974	136	74	62	118	71	47
1975	151	84	67	129	65	64
1976	139	80	59	121	81	40
1977	140	81	59	114	79	35
1978	137	74	63	120	63	57
1979	130	72	58	114	63	51
1980	124	65	59	103	64	39
1981	119	62	57	104	55	49
1982	114	65	49	97	51	46
1983	114	66	48	100	59	41
1984	113	66	47	90	53	37
1985	107	59	48	95	53	42
1986	105	62	43	93	54	39
1987	104	61	43	86	54	32
1988	102	62	40	84	51	33
1989	98	58	40	80	43	37
1990	86	50	36	70	37	33
1991	87	53	34	65	42	23
1992	85	53	32	66	42	24
1993	82	45	37	66	38	28
1994	80	52	28	64	48	16
1995	80	48	32	61	43	18
1996	77	46	31	60	39	21
1997	77	45	32	58	40	18
1998	77	45	32	59	40	19
1999	75	44	31	58	39	19
2000	74	44	30	56	38	18
2001	72	42	30	54	35	19
2002	69	40	29	50	32	18
2003	66	38	28	48	31	17
2004	64	40	24	45	35	10

Source: Computed from SRS Bulletins, Registrar General, New Delhi, India.

from 2002. IMR in Tamil Nadu has reached the level of 49 in 2001 and 43 in 2003. Congenital malformations and genetic disorders have become the third most common cause of mortality in newborns in India.

The infant mortality rate for Rural India was 72/1000 and for Urban India it was 42/1000. For Tamil Nadu the same was 54/1000 and 35/1000 respectively. While IMR for Scheduled Castes at All India Level was 83/1000, for Scheduled Tribes it was 84.2/1000 and for other Disadvantaged Group it was 76/1000. The factors, which influence infant and neonatal deaths, are socio-economic status, level of health care

Table 4
Health Status of the Socially Marginalised Groups

	Infant Mortality/ 1000	*Under-5 Mortality/ 1000*	*% Children Underweight*
India	70	94.9	47
Scheduled Caste	83	119.3	53.5
Scheduled Tribes	84.2	126.6	55.9
Other Disadvantaged	76	103.1	47.3
Others	61.8	82.6	41.1

Source: National Health Policy, 2001.

provision, population movement, parental age, parental smoking, occupational exposures, exposure to drug, nutritional status and consanguinity. Among the socially marginalized weaker sections of the society, poverty, illiteracy coupled with existing caste and dowry system have resulted in the preference for consanguineous marriages leading to adverse health effects in children.

Prevalence of Consanguineous Marriages in India and Tamil Nadu

A marriage is said to be consanguineous when the union is between two people related by descent from a common ancestor. Consanguineous marriages depend on factors like demographic, socio-cultural, socio-economic, religious, geographic conditions and societal life pattern. All these factors are inter-linked with each other.

In Northern parts of India, Hindus prohibit consanguineous marriages which dates back to approximately 200 B.C. In Northern India, Aryans prohibit marriages up to seven generations on the male side and five generations on the female side.[5]

The Dravidian Hindus of South India strongly favour marriage between first cousins and particularly in the States of Andhra Pradesh, Karnataka and Tamil Nadu uncle-niece marriages are widely practised. The most frequent type of marriages among the Hindus in Southern India is cross-cousin marriages. Hindus prohibit parallel cousin marriages in both North and South India. In South India, uncle-niece marriage is also commonly practised. The Hindu Marriage Act of 1955 bans uncle-niece marriage but it has been relaxed where custom allows it.

In India, there is a lack of proper single database on the prevalence rate of consanguineous marriages. Based on the advice of J.B.S. Haldane,[6] the prevalence rate of consanguineous marriage was collected along with 1961 Census. In 1992-93, National Family Health Survey-1 undertook a National representative survey and it collected information on the rate of prevalence of consanguineous marriages in various States of India. This Survey estimated the prevalence and the pattern of consanguinity.

NFHS-1 collected data from both urban and rural respondents whereas in 1960 Survey data were collected only from villages. In both the Surveys, the highest percentage rates of consanguineous marriages were in Southern States of Andhra Pradesh (36.2 and 30.8), Karnataka (30.2 and 29.7) and Tamil Nadu (31.1 and 38.2).

Table 5
Consanguineous Marriage in India by State, 1960 and 1992-93

Region	*1960*		*NFHS-1 1992-93*	
State	*Consanguineous Marriages (%)*	*Mean Co-efficient of Inbreeding*	*Consanguineous Marriages (%)*	*Mean Co-efficient of Inbreeding*
NORTH				
Delhi	-	-	4.3	0.0023
Haryana	-	-	1.0	0.0004
Himachal Pradesh	0.1	0.0006	0.8	0.003
Jammu & Kashmir	15.5	0.0098	8.0	0.0049
Punjab	1.1	0.0007	0.9	0.0006
Rajasthan	21.0	0.0132	1.3	0.0006
CENTRAL				
Madhya Pradesh	3.2	0.0021	4.1	0.0025
Uttar Pradesh	3.3	0.0020	7.5	0.0044
EAST				
Bihar	2.7	0.0018	5.0	0.0032
Orissa	8.3	0.0054	5.7	0.0035
West Bengal	0.2	0.0001	5.0	0.0030
NORTH EAST				
Arunachal Pradesh	3.4	0.0025	3.9	0.0029
Assam	1.4	0.0010	1.7	0.0010
Manipur	10.6	0.0066	2.1	0.0013
Meghalaya	-	-	2.7	0.0018
Mizoram	-	-	0.5	0.002
Nagaland	-	-	1.5	0.009
Tripura	-	-	1.9	0.0010
WEST				
Goa	-	-	10.6	0.0066
Gujarat	9.2	0.0058	4.9	0.0029
Maharashtra	21.2	0.0147	21.0	0.0131
SOUTH				
Andhra Pradesh	36.2	0.0250	30.8	0.0212
Karnataka	30.2	0.0256	29.7	0.0180
Kerala	17.4	0.107	7.5	0.0042
Tamil Nadu	31.1	0.0228	38.2	0.0266
ALL INDIA	12.9	0.0095	11.9	0.0075

Source: Bittles, A.H. (2002), "The Impact of Consanguinity on Indian Population", *Indian Journal of Human Genetics*, Vol. 8, Issue-2, pp. 45-51.

Wide variations are found among the Southern States. The frequency of consanguinity varied from 52 per cent in Tamil Nadu to approximately 37 per cent in Andhra Pradesh and Karnataka, and to only 11 per cent in Kerala. (Banerjee and Roy, 1996).[7] Consanguineous marriages are regarded as customary for South Indians, which was confirmed in the Hindu Code Bill of 1984.

Table 6 depicts the calculated mean in-breeding co-efficient for Most Backward Communities as 0.0557, followed by Scheduled Castes with 0.0554, for Backward Communities with 0.0469 and for Other Castes with 0.0458. This shows that economically backward and vulnerable communities married their relatives than Other communities, due to poverty resulting in high congenital disorders in these communities.

Table 6

Co-efficient of Consanguinity for Different Caste Groups

SL.No	*Relationship*	*O.C*	*B.C*	*M.BC*	*S.C*	*S.T*
1.	Uncle -Niece	0.0416	0.0340	0.0375	0.0409	0.0156
2.	First Cousins	0.0034	0.0110	0.0171	0.0129	0.0078
3.	Second Cousins	0.0008	0.0019	0.0011	0.0016	-
	Total Consanguineous Marriages	0.0458	0.0469	0.0557	0.0554	0.0234

Source: Usha Rani (2006), "Economics of Child Health: A Study with Reference to Consanguinity and Congenital Disorders in Chennai City, Tamil Nadu", pp. 216

Reasons for High Prevalence of Consanguineous Marriages

Consanguineous marriages largely depend on geographic, demographic and economic factors. Socio-economic status has a large impact on the level of consanguinity. The poorest and the least educated people in a society tend to have the highest level of consanguinity. Economic considerations are important in communities where either dowry or bride wealth payments are the norms. The arrangement of a marriage within the family reduces or sometimes even abolishes the associated financial costs. In a country where more than 260 million population live below the poverty line, and with existence of century old dowry system, people favour consanguineous marriages.

The most vulnerable groups of the society especially in rural areas and urban slums commonly practise consanguineous marriage. The existence of poverty and unemployment are also the root cause for such marriages. The socially and economically backward groups find their mates within their family clans.

Effects of Consanguinity on Child Health - Congenital Disorders

Consanguinity leads to infant, peri-natal, neonatal mortality, stillbirth and congenital disorders in the offspring of consanguineous parents. In India, congenital and hereditary genetic diseases are becoming a significant health burden. Congenital anomalies account for eight to 15 per cent of peri-natal deaths and 13 to 16 per cent of neonatal deaths in India.[8] With improved control of infection and nutritional deficiencies, congenital malformations have become an important cause of peri-natal mortality. With a very large population, high birth rate and consanguineous marriages favoured in many communities, there is high prevalence of genetic disorders in India.

According to Table 7 the incidence of congenital malformation is 1:49, which makes congenital disorders to be the most important cause of Neonatal and Peri-natal deaths in India. Neural Tube Defects (NTDs) is the most common malformation observed among newborns in India.

Table 7
Burden of Genetic Disease at Birth in India

Disorder	*Incidence*	*Number / Year*
Congenital Malformations	1:49	495,096
Down Syndrome	1:1139	21,412
Beta-thalassaemia	1:2700	9,000
Sickle Cell Disease	-	5,200
Metabolic Disorders	1:2497	9,760

Source: Talukdar, Geeta and Sharma, Archana (2006), "Genetic Causes of Congenital Malformation in India", *International Journal of Human Genetics*, Vol. 6(1), pp. 5-25.

Congenital malformations are not considered as priority health problem in India and importance is given to infection and malnutrition than congenital disorders. However, in view of the fact that congenital malformations contribute significantly to neonatal mortality and morbidity and physical handicap in later life, there is the need to give serious consideration to these problem

SUGGESTIONS

- There is greater need to inform, educate, and communicate people about the ill-effects of the consanguineous marriages and its resultant congenital disorders.
- Given the wide spread practice of close marriages in Tamil Nadu across all socio-economic groups, there is the need to validate the findings in less educated and economically disadvantageous slum population sub-groups in different parts of the State.
- Efficient surveillance systems, Registries and database are the basis for successful public programmes. Therefore, it is necessary to maintain efficient registering system in hospitals about consanguinity and congenital disorders in order to have a continued research in the field of health economics.

- Peri-natal screening should be encouraged in pregnancies at an early stage itself to avoid such unpleasant births. Government should take necessary steps to provide this facility to all sections of the community at a cheaper cost.
- It is necessary on the part of the Health Department of the Government to provide necessary infrastructure to identify and treat the health problems of the neonates so that the high percentage of early neonatal mortality can be reduced considerably.

NOTES

1. Lawn, Joy; Katanrzyna, Wikzynska - Ketende and Cousens, Simon (2006), "Estimating the Causes of 4 Million Neonatal Deaths in the year 2000", *International Journal of Epidemiology*, Vol. 35, No. 3, pp. 706-18.
2. UNICEF: The State of the World's Children 2005, Childhood Under Threat, December, 2004, pp. 4-15.
3. Tenth Five Year Plan (2002-2007), Millennium Development Goals.
4. Dr. Chandramouli, Director of Census Operation, Tamil Nadu (2002), "Infant Mortality: No Room for Complacency", THE HINDU, July, 16.
5. Kapadia, K.M. (1958), "Marriage and Family in India", Oxford University Press, Calcutta, Second Edition, pp.117-37.
6. Choudhary, Roy, A.K. (1976), "Incidence of Inbreeding in Different States of India", Demography of India, Vol.No.5, pp.108-15.
7. Sushanta K. Banerjee and Roy, T.K. (2002), "Parental Consanguinity and Off Spring Mortality: The Search for Possible Linkage in the Indian Context", Asia-Pacific Population Journal, March, Vol.17, No.1, pp.17-24.
8. Agarwal, S.S.; Singh, U. and Singh, P.S. (1991), "Prevalence and Spectrum of Congenital Malformations in a Prospective Study at a Teaching Hospital", Indian Journal of Medical Research, Vol.94, pp.413-9.

REFERENCES

Census of India, "Population Projections for India and States, 2001-2026", Report of the Technical Group on Population Projections, National Commission on Population, New Delhi, India, May, 2006.

Christianson, Arnald; Hawson, P. Christopher and Modell, B., (2006), "Global Report on Birth Defects: The Hidden Toll of Dying and Disabled Children", March of Dimes Birth Defects Foundation, White Plains, New York.

IIPS (1999), National Family and Health Survey-2, 1998-99, International Institute for Population Sciences, Bombay, India.

Planning Commission, Millennium Development Goals, Tenth Five-Year Plan (2002-2007).

Sample Registration System, Bulletins, (2006), Office of the Registrar General, New Delhi, India.

UNICEF, (2006), "Childhood Under Threat", The State of the World's Children 2005, December.

WHO, (2005), The World Health Report, Make Every Mother and Child Count, Geneva.

WHO, New Born Deaths: WHO Draft Neonatal Peri-natal Estimates as of January, 2005, Supplemental data for 25 countries from ORSMauo/DHS 2000-2005 Save the Children.

4

RURAL–URBAN DISPARITY IN EDUCATION

LEELA BHASKAR

INTRODUCTION

While India's national economy booms, educational disparity between rural and urban areas remains a major issue of concern, specifically in terms of resources, infrastructure, and funding. Despite the Indian government's attempts at ameliorating the problem through increased rural education funding and targeted programs such as the *Mid-Day Meals Scheme*, illiteracy levels in rural India remain alarmingly high.

Between 1954 and 1974 enrolment into primary education and literacy attainment had doubled. Provision of school meals, free text books, and trained teachers has helped to improve the quality of education. Literacy has been linked to extension through the Farmers Functional Literacy Programme. But there are glaring disparities between rural and urban rates of wastage and literacy. Efforts to improve the situation should give priority to (1) the rural areas, and (2) within rural areas to the scheduled castes and scheduled tribes, and (3) within these two, to women. Current policy links universal primary education and adult literacy and this will involve increasing the financial allocation to primary education at the expense of higher education and a 100% increase in the allocation to adult education.

There is also a lack of proper infrastructure in a lot of rural areas be it with regards to the building or staff. Where there has been a huge amount of progress in this field ever since independence, there is still a lot of work to be done - Several programmes have been put forward by governments from time for the proper implementation of primary education. It includes District Primary Education Programme (DPEP) in 1992, the Minimum Levels of Learning (MLL) initiative and more recently the Sarva Shiksha Abhiyan (or the National Programme for Universal Elementary Education).

The development of primary schools in India differs from place to place. Some states in India like Kerala, Tamilnadu stand in the forefront where as states like Bihar remains largely underdeveloped in this aspect. The northeast states also fall short of proper implementation of primary education policies. Primary schools in India, with sincere and continuous efforts by governments, NGOs and other communities, India's primary schools are gaining a lot of momentum. Such basic facilities like drinking water facilities, toilet facilities, proper classrooms and qualified staff are being emphasized on. In the urban areas constant innovations are carried out in teaching methods and subjects so as to improve.

Eradication of illiteracy has been one of the major national concerns of the Government of India since independence. A number of significant programmes have been taken up since Independence to eradicate illiteracy among adults. Some of the important programmes included:

- Social Education - implemented in the First Five-Year Plan (1951-56). The programme gave importance to literacy, extension, general education, leadership training and social consciousness.
- 'Gram Shikshan Mohim' - a movement for literacy in the rural areas started first in Satara district of Maharashtra in 1959 which was later extended to other parts of the state. The programme aimed at imparting basic literacy skills within a period of four months.
- Farmer's Functional Literacy Project (FFLP) - started in 1967-68 as an inter-ministerial project for farmers' training and functional literacy. The project aimed at popularisation of high yielding varieties of seeds through the process of adult education in 144 districts.
- Non-formal education (NFE) - launched in the beginning of Fifth Five Year Plan for the age group of 15-25 years.
- Functional Literacy for Adult Women (FLAW) - started in 1975-76 in the experimental Integrated Child Development Scheme (ICDS) project areas. The scheme included a component which enabled illiterate adult women to acquire functional skills along with literacy, to gain better awareness of health, hygiene, child care practices and in the process facilitated attitudinal changes.
- National Adult Education Programme (NAEP) - launched on October, 2 1978. This was the first programme in India taken up at macro level to eradicate illiteracy through project approach. It was a massive programme aimed at educating 100 million non-literate adults in the age-group of 15-35 years within a time frame of five years.

- Rural Functional Literacy Project (RFLP) - the objectives of the scheme were: to impart functional literacy to all illiterate persons in 15-35 age group who are living in the rural areas by organising specified number of literacy centres in accordance with the norms and guidelines issued by the then Department of Education, Ministry of HRD from time to time.
- Mass Programme of Functional Literacy (MPFL) - launched on May 1, 1986 by involving National Service Scheme (NSS) and other students in colleges and universities. During 1987-88, NCC Cadets from senior division were also involved in the programme.

Tamil Nadu is geographically the 11th largest state in India with an area of 130,058 square kilometres accounting for 4% of the national area. It has a long coastline extending up to 1000 kms. Climatically the state falls into a semi - humid and a semi - arid zone. As per Census 2001, Tamil Nadu is one of the better off states in India in terms of high overall literacy rate of 73% and also a high female literacy rate of about 65%. Thus, an inquiry into the existing primary education service and its distinguishing features in the state becomes relevant.Tamil Nadu has an impressive coverage of habitations in rural areas with schooling facilities at primary stage within one kilometre. In 2005, 99% of rural habitations had already been covered.

In Tamil Nadu, statistics show a huge drop in the number of Higher Secondary Schools available in the state as compared to the available

Table 1
Type of Schools and Enrolment in Tamil Nadu, 2005-06

		All Areas			*Rural Areas*		
Type of Schools	*Govt. or Pvt.*	*Schools*	*Enrolment*	*Average Enrolment Per School*	*Schools*	*Enrolment*	*Average Enrolment Per School*
Primary only	Govt.	24201	2222427	91.8	22640	1974234	87.2
	Pvt.	9715	1491522	153.5	6585	819920	124.5
Primary with UP	Govt.	6534	1683155	257.6	5857	1438460	245.6
	Pvt.	2580	1036805	401.9	1673	567841	339.4
Primary, UP & HS	Govt.	2146	577228	269.0	1914	505095	263.9
	Pvt.	2307	686184	297.4	1350	365721	270.9
UP only	Govt.	1658	714874	431.2	1307	530183	405.6
	Pvt.	2432	1342502	552.0	1014	466609	460.2
UP & HS	Govt.	0	0	-	0	0	-
	Pvt.	1	0	-	1	0	-
No response	Govt.	0	0	-	0	0	-
	Pvt.	0	0	-	0	0	-

Note: *P*=Primary; *UP*=Upper Primary; *HS*=Higher Secondary; Govt.=Government; Pvt.=Private

Source: State Report Card 2006

number of primary schools. Not to forget the unequal distribution of schools between the urban and the rural areas. Hence the children are forced to drop out of school because the nearest middle school would be so many kms away. And the parents are apprehensive about sending their children too far away from home, when they could be of some use at home, or earn money for the family. Child labour and early marriages are two very dangerous outputs of the dropout issue. In Andhra Pradesh almost 80% of girl children are married.

The additional requirement of financial resources is Rs. 4.5 billion in Tamil Nadu to scale up the rural services in primary education. On a per capita basis, this works out to Rs.67. While rural Tamil Nadu has already the physical infrastructure in place, it requires some additional effort to maintain and improve the existing infrastructure. Tamil Nadu is placed far better than the northern states like UP, MP and Rajasthan in terms of physical infrastructure or even the southern states, such as Karnataka and Andhra Pradesh. This is not surprising because the state has been spending considerably higher amounts per capita than most states for the past several years. In 2007-08 budget, Tamil Nadu allocated Rs.84.3 billion or Rs.1,260 per capita. The additional effort required as per our estimate is, therefore, only 5.3% over two years. It is definitely not a very tough target for the state to achieve.

Table 2
Selected Characteristics of Schools in Tamil Nadu, 2005-06

Sr.No.	*Characteristics*	*Type of Schools*			
		Only P	*P+UP*	*P+UP+HS*	*Only UP*
1	% of Single classroom schools	7.6	0.7	1.1	0.3
2	% of Schools with *pucca* Buildings	54.3	41.7	62.1	60.6
3	% of Schools with No Buildings	0.05	0.0	0.01	0.0
4	% of Enrol. in Schools w/o Buildings	0.0	0.0	0.1	0.0
5	% of Schools with Girls' Toilets	44.7	66.5	83.8	84.9
6	% of Schools w/o Toilets	42.8	43.1	53.9	49.6
7	% of Single Teacher Schools	4.7	0.5	1.3	0.7
8	% of Enrol. In Single Teacher Schools	2.1	0.2	0.6	0.2
9	% of Schools with SCR>60*	4.3	9.0	6.6	5.6
10	% of Enrol. In Schools with SCR>60*	10.9	16.6	27.7	0.2
11	% of Enrol. In Schools w/o Blackboard	3.1	3.0	5.7	6.8
12	% of No Female Teacher Schools	10.1	4.6	4.0	2.6
13	% of Schools with Pre-primary Section	16.9	12.3	31.3	0.0
14	% of Girls' Enrolment	48.7	48.7	48.2	46.7
15	% of Schools with Students < = 50	35.1	1.9	3.2	3.1
16	% Schools with PTR > 100*	0.5	1.4	2.5	2.6
17	% of Schools Established since 1994	15.0	6.8	36.8	11.9

**Note:* SCR = Students Classroom Ratio; PTR = Pupil Teacher Ratio
Source: Same as Table 1.

Physical infrastructure in terms of classrooms and their quality is important in attracting pupils to school. Table 3 provides the data in this regard by types of schools. Only primary schools in Tamil Nadu have on an average about 4.17 classrooms. Only 7.6% of the schools have a single classroom. If these schools run in two shifts, the problem of multiple standards using the same classroom simultaneously may be easily solved. This can ensure quality education. Moreover, these classrooms are also not in good condition in the state. Almost 18% of the classrooms require minor repairs and about 5% require major repairs. Thus, although new schools and new buildings may not be required in big number in the state, significant repairs besides additional rooms needs to be constructed.

Table 3
Classrooms and Their Conditions by Types of School, Tamil Nadu 2005-06

Sr.No.	*Specifications*	*Type of Schools*				
		Only P	*P+UP*	*P+UP+HS*	*Only UP*	*UP+HS*
1	No. of schools	33916	9114	4453	4090	1
2	No. of classrooms (CR)	141536	81077	48630	91403	1
3	No. of other rooms	26254	14817	15385	24809	0
4	No. of CR needing Minor Repair	24910	12972	4425	7769	0
5	No. of CR needing Major Repair	7077	4540	1362	3473	0
6	Av. No. of CR per school	4.2	8.9	10.9	22.3	1

Source: Same as Table 1.

Another major problem with existing primary schools in Tamil Nadu is of availability of teachers in general and of female teachers in particular. Table 4 provides teacher related relevant data for schools in rural area.

Table 4
Teachers in Rural Schools, Tamil Nadu 2005-06

Sr. No.	*Specification*	*Type of Schools*				
		Only P	*P+UP*	*P+UP+HS*	*Only UP*	*UP+HS*
1	No. of Teachers in Govt. schools	67103	44300	18724	32529	0
2	No. of Teachers in Pvt. schools.	56205	31806	27966	51312	3
3	No. of Regular Teachers	121960	75574	45739	82123	3
4	No. of Para Teachers	1348	532	951	17180	
5	No. of Total Teachers	123308	76106	46690	83841	3
6	% of Trained Teachers (Males)	84.9	69.4	37.9	31.80	
7	% of Trained Teachers (Females)	63.1	68.5	27.5	27.70	
8	Regular Teachers Per School (Govt.)	2.7	6.7	8.5	19.30	
9	Regular Teachers Per School (Pvt.)	5.8	12.3	11.9	20.63	
10	Enrol. Per Regular Teacher (Govt.)	30.0	32.8	27.6	16.60	
11	Enrol. Per Regular Teacher (Pvt.)	14.6	17.9	13.3	9.30	

Note: *P*=Primary; *UP*=Upper Primary; *HS*=Higher Secondary; Govt.=Government; Pvt.=Private

Source: Same as Table 1.

It can be seen from the *Table 4* that average number of regular teachers in government primary schools in rural Tamil Nadu is only 2.7. Single teacher Primary Schools are only about 4.7% (see *Table 2*), which includes private schools and primary schools in urban areas, too. Since government schools are known to have less number of teachers in rural areas as compared to the private schools, it implies that a majority of the government primary schools in rural Tamil Nadu have only two regular teachers. Thus, although the government primary schools in rural Tamil Nadu have about three to four classrooms, there are only two regular teachers with 5 standards running simultaneously. These schools therefore, somewhat lack a proper learning environment and the quality of education suffers as a result. The student-teacher ratio, which is on an average 30 in government primary schools of Tamil Nadu, is also not very favourable. The table clearly brings out that the physical learning environment indicators are far better for the private primary schools. It is not surprising if parents prefer to send their children to private schools. It only shows that parents highly value educational quality and learning environment provided to their children. For any exercise of scaling up rural primary education services, the teacher-school ratio, student-teacher ratio and classroom-school ratio cannot be ignored. Rural Tamil Nadu faces problems on at least two of these three fronts. The transition rate, however, of primary to upper primary level for students in Tamil Nadu is as high as 92% and very low dropout rate.

The standard response of the government to reduce drop-out rate, increase attendance, retention, and transition rates is to provide incentives to children besides free education and the mid-day meal schemes. Accordingly the government of Tamil Nadu provides various incentives in terms of providing free textbooks, stationery, uniform and attendance related incentives for the children in the primary and upper primary government schools. Table 5 provides the number of beneficiary children in the primary and upper primary schools in Tamil Nadu in 2005-06.

In Tamil Nadu, textbooks are distributed free to all children in the primary and the upper primary classes. Stationery like notebooks, pencil, eraser, etc. is distributed free to children belonging to SC/ST.

Table 5
Number of Beneficiaries of Various Incentives, Tamil Nadu,2005-06

Incentives	*Primary*		*Upper Primary*	
	Boys	*Girls*	*Boys*	*Girls*
Text-Books	2539471	2428604	1764213	1649375
Stationery	316488	361950	426497	431966
Attendance	17808	68817	130212	148874
Uniform	1990119	1891938	959832	903430

Source: Same as Table 1.

As a second step, the crucial 4 parameters (ratios), *viz.*, enrolment per classroom (E/CR); classrooms per school (CR/S); teachers per classroom (T/CR); and enrolment per teacher (E/T). For physical quantity of infrastructure and quality of primary education, these four parameters are very important. Their existing and desirable average values in rural Tamil Nadu are presented in Table 6.

Table 6 addresses the basic problems of primary educational services in rural areas of Tamil Nadu. Government schools in Tamil Nadu are close to the desirable values in enrolment per classroom as well as classrooms per school. However, the availability of teachers per classroom is lower than the desirable values. In order to improve the quality of primary education in Tamil Nadu, considered these aspects while fixing the targets for the parameter values.

Table 6
Selected Parameter Values for Rural Tamil Nadu, 2005-06

Values	*Enrol./CR*	*CR/School*	*Teachers/CR*	*Enrol./Teacher*
Existing Values	25.25	5.17	1.05	24.07
Desirable Values	26	5	1.18	22

Source: Tables 1, 3, and 4 above; and our discussions and Survey, 2008

Table 7 provides our estimates of the gap between the required and existing levels of services in primary education in the rural areas of the state. This is done in two steps: (1) estimating the gap in 2005-06 with existing values of parameters; and (2) estimating the gap in 2009-10 with desired (target) values of parameters.

Rural areas of Tamil Nadu do not have severe shortfall in terms of physical facilities and access of population to primary education. The problem is more in terms of improving the quality of services in public schools. The basic physical infrastructural facilities like water, electricity, classrooms, toilets, etc., are very important determinants of the learning

Table 7
Estimates of Gap in Levels of Primary Education Services in Rural Areas of Tamil Nadu

Sr.No	*Year*	*Schools*	*Enrolment*	*Teachers*	*Classrooms*
1	2005-06 (Existing)	36755	4800455	199414	190150
2	2005-06 (Required with existing Parameters)	37541	4903081	203677	194215
3	2005-06 (Gap = (2) - (1))	786	102626	4263	4065
4	2009-10 (Required with Desired Parameters)	38938	5061873	230085	194687
5	2009-10 (Gap = (4) - (1)	2183	261418	30671	4537

Table 8
Additional Expenditure Requirement for Scaling-up Rural Primary Education in Tamil Nadu

Sr. No.	*Item*	*Remarks/Details*	*Unit Cost (Rs.000)*	*No. of Units Required*	*Cost in Rs. Million*
1	Classrooms	Average unit cost including extension	105.84	4,537	480
2	New schools + toilets + furniture classrooms	Furniture – Rs.15,000* Toilets – Rs.32,000* Existing school w/o building	116.9	2,183+ 15	255+1.7
3	Major repairs	Per classroom	22.1	9,923	714
4	Minor repairs	Per classroom	11	32,358	109
5	Toilets	1 unit = 1 boys' + 1 girls'	33.1	15,754	521
	Total Capital Cost		-	2,081	
6	Maintenance	Utilities + colour + garden	16.5	38,938	642
7	Regular Teacher	New Regular teachers @ Rs.11,000 p.m.	132	2,183	288
8	Para-Teachers	@ Rs.3,000 pm	36	28,488	1026
9	Teaching contingency	To each teacher	0.55	30,671	17
10	Training stipend	For Regular Teachers			
	-Regular Teachers	@ Rs.100 for 20 days/year.	2.0	2,183	4
	- Para Teachers	@ Rs.100 for 30 days/year	3.0	28,488	85
11	Helper	Cleaning, gardening, cooking and general	6.62	38,938	258
12	Textbook + stationary	To all students	0.11	261,418	29
13	Scholarship	To all BPL and SC+ST+ OBC students	0.33	104,567	35
	Total Recurring Cost	2,384			
	Total cost		4,465		
	Per Capita basis	66.89mn is estimated rural population of TN for (October) 20009-10 (Per capita cost in Rs.)	-		31
	-Capital Cost		-		36
	-Recurring Cost		-		67
	-Total Cost		-		67
	Total Cost	-	-		

Note: *Formula unit for school includes 3 tables + 6 chairs + 3 cupboards + 3 wooden blackboard + 4 hanging blackboard; and toilet unit include 1 toilet each for boys and girls.

Source: Tables 1, 2, 3,4,and 7 and our Survey, 2008.

environment. All such facilities need to be adequately and urgently provided. This requires a multi-departmental or "integrated" approach. If coordination among education, health, power, construction (PWD), roads, transport departments, is not possible at a higher level, education department will have to take responsibility of all these activities and provide a comprehensive solution.

The disparity between the rural and urban school and college students is only increasing by the day. While the students studying in city have the advantage of quality teachers and greater exposure and as a result are well informed, their counterparts in remote villages do not have the same exposure. The drop-out rate in primary and upper primary schools in Tamil Nadu was also among the lowest in India. The dropout rate in primary schools fell from 4 percent in 2006-07 to 1.2 percent. Tamil Nadu recorded close to 100 percent Gross Enrolment Ratio (GER) at primary and upper primary levels. Rural areas of Tamil Nadu do not have any severe shortfall in terms of physical facilities and access of population to primary education is pretty good. The problem, however, is more in terms of improving the quality of services being provided in public schools.

The millennium development goal about literacy is to make primary education universal. The net enrolment rate in the population 6-11 years should be made 100%. For our purpose, it becomes an effective target for scaling up effort. Besides, the quality of the inputs should also improve to deliver the service with outcome orientation. The Census of India, 2001 provides population of states by rural-urban residence and five year age-groups. By making appropriate adjustments and assuming the annual growth rates of 0.8% for rural Tamil Nadu we get 4.9031 million children in the age-group 6-11 years in October 2005 and 5.0619 million in October 2009.

REFERENCES

Bajpai, Nirupam, Ravindra Dholakia and Jeffrey D. Sachs. (2008), 'Scaling up Primary Education Services in Rural India: Case Studies of Andhra Pradesh and Karnataka', Center on Globalization and Sustainable Development, Columbia University, Working Paper No. 34, New York.

Banerji, Rukmini (2003), 'Making the Grade: Teach Children the Joy of Learning.' Times of India, July 14, New Delhi.

Dholakia, Ravindra H. and Iyengar Shreekant (2008), "Access of Poor to Primary Education in Rural India", *appearing in Journal of Educational Planning and Administration*.

Kumar, Sanjay, et. al. (2003), Primary Education in Rural Areas - An Alternative Model, Economic and Political Weekly, August 23-29.

Planning Commission (2006a), Towards Faster and More Inclusive Growth - An Approach to the 11th Five Year Plan, Govt. of India, June 14. (Referred to as "Approach Paper to 11th Plan"). (*http://planningcommission.nic.in*)

Ramachandran, Vimla, (2005), Why School Teachers are Demotivated and Disheartened, *Economic and Political Weekly*, May 21-27.

State Report Card 2006, National University of Educational Planning and Administration. (*www.depemis.org*)

Tamil Nadu Human Development Report (2003), Government of Tamil Nadu. (*http://www.tn.gov.in*).

5

SOCIAL DISPARITY IN EDUCATIONAL ATTAINMENT: A MICRO LEVEL STUDY

N. Palani Raj

INTRODUCTION

The role of economic factors and their influence on educational decisions of families is widely acknowledged as it is treated as an investment. Especially in the rural context, under conditions of socio-economic deprivation, costs and benefits of this 'investment' are rationally analyzed in terms of two aspects:

- Expectations of benefits, which may be economic and non-economic in nature.
- The ability of families to sustain both the direct and indirect costs involved in schooling.

The absence of any of these could lead to a situation of educational deprivation characterized by non-enrolment, irregular attendance and discontinuance. Conversely, it has also been found that economic well being facilitates this process of schooling. In order to understand the exact role played by the socio-economic factors in determining access and retention of children in schools among different social groups, a micro level study has been attempted with the help of primary household level data.

REVIEW OF LITERATURE

Per Capita Income

The income group a family belongs to co-relates with enrolment. Enrolment and participation rates are lower for low- income families, while greater household wealth enhances school participation of both boys and girls. Filmer and Pritchett showed that there is a strong wealth effect on the probability of enrolment. All else being equal, a child from a household from the highest quintile is 31 percentage points more likely to be in school than a child from a poor quintile *(Filmer & Pritchett 1999)*.

Land Owning Patterns

Land owning status, which is the main determinant of economic position in rural areas, exerts a great influence on enrolment as can be seen by higher enrolments among families with larger land holdings. Children of families with small / marginal land holdings face a problem, as their children are often withdrawn to work on land *(Reddy Shiva et al., 1992).*

Nature of Occupation

Pandey and Talwar's study of Andhra Pradesh finds that, a village where the majority of population depends on non-agriculture for their livelihood was one of the best enrolled villages at all levels of education. It was found that fathers working as agricultural labourers have the largest percentage of illiterate children while fathers in service had lowest. Also, children of agricultural labourers often had to discontinue schooling to engage in some job for improving the economic status of the family *(Pandey and Talwar 1980).*

Role of Poverty

The fact that poverty is a hindrance to schooling should not be looked at in absolute terms. Inter-regional variations in educational achievements between Uttar Pradesh and Kerala, for instance, show that while both the states had an average of 45%, people below the poverty line, Kerala had a literacy rate of 90%, while UP's literacy rate was only 40.5% *(Bhatty 1998).* Other empirical studies also show that among the very poor landless labourers, in poor economic conditions, parents send their children to school more easily, as they are not needed for productive work on the farm.

Caste

Apart from class distinctions, it has also been found that, caste, tribe and gender gaps in school participation of children are also exacerbated by poverty.

In the highly stratified rural Indian context, the poorer sections are also those which form the bulk of the lower castes, such as the Scheduled Castes (SCs) and Scheduled Tribes (STs). Social exclusion and discrimination, together with landlessness and poverty, combine to keep them out of the sphere of education.

DROP OUT AND LITERACY LEVEL: A MACRO PICTURE

The Tapas Majumdar Committee Report (1999) has estimated the size of out of school children to be about 60-70 million. The NSSO data on out of school children aged between 5-14 years, reveals that while the percentage of those who never attended is small, the percentage of those who dropped out is alarmingly high. Vast variations exist between states in their efforts to provide eight years of elementary schooling. The spread of education has been uneven not only in terms of inter-state variations, but also between rural and urban areas, with urban areas being at an advantage compared to the rural areas. Social inequalities of caste, class and gender have manifested themselves in primary school participation and completion, as a result of which, certain segments of society, such as the SCs, STs, and girls in rural areas, have continued to lag behind the general population.

Table 1
All India: Percentage of out-of-school Children in the Age Group of 5-14, NSS 55th Round, 2004-05

Social Group	*Dropped Out*			*Never Attended*		
Rural Male	*5-9*	*10-14*	*5-14*	*5-9*	*10-14*	*5-14*
SC	36.1	28.5	32.7	4.0	2.9	3.5
ST	42.5	35.8	39.4	3.2	3.1	3.1
Others	26.8	18.2	22.6	3.7	2.7	3.2
All	30.4	22.0	26.4	3.7	2.8	3.3
Urban Male						
SC	24.9	15.1	20.1	2.1	3.4	2.7
ST	19.3	17.1	18.3	3.4	3.2	3.3
Others	12.3	11.2	11.8	2.6	1.9	2.2
All	14.4	11.9	13.2	2.5	2.1	2.3
Rural Female						
SC	48.4	51.6	49.9	4.3	4.1	4.2
ST	55.9	55.8	55.9	4.0	3.2	3.7
Others	35.6	36.4	36.0	3.9	3.4	3.7
All	40.5	41.3	40.8	4.0	3.5	3.8
Urban Female						
SC	29.0	28.0	28.5	3.1	3.2	3.2
ST	30.8	21.1	25.9	5.2	4.6	4.9
Others	15.1	14.7	14.9	2.9	2.8	2.8
All	17.6	16.6	17.1	3.0	2.9	3.0

Source: NSSO, 2006.

Caste

Census, NSSO and NCAER data all show that members of Schedule Castes and Schedule Tribes, who have been historically disadvantaged socially, economically and educationally, have had lower school participation in terms of enrolment and retention compared to the general population. The 1981 and 1991 census data shows that crude literacy rates for both men and women belonging to SC and ST were significantly lower compared to the general population.

Data available from census and surveys clearly point out that SC and ST children have lower school attendance and higher drop out rates compared to the general population. According to the 1991 census, less than 50% of SC male children were attending school in Andhra Pradesh, Bihar, Rajasthan, Madhya Pradesh and West Bengal. Among SC girls, the proportion attending school was less than 50% in all of the states except Himachal Pradesh, Tamil Nadu, Kerala and Gujarat. NSSO data on out-of-school children show that dropouts are much higher among rural girls of SC and ST communities, when compared to the general population. Approximately 50% of SC and 56% of ST girls dropped out of school compared to 36% from the 'others' category.

DROP OUT AND LITERACY LEVEL: A MICRO LEVEL STUDY

The basic objective of this study is to analyse the problems of the drop out children in the Cheyyar taluk in Tiruvannamalai district with the help of primary data. For this purpose, data have been collected from 80 sample households, residing in various places like slum, villages and also towns of this taluk.

Community and Educational Levels

The social traits of the respondents include community of the households, since community plays a pivotal role in enabling or disabling a person in attaining a particular level of education. Hence, it is pertinent to analyse the community and educational level-wise distribution of the sample respondents, which is done with the help of Table 1a.

Table 1a
Community and Educational Levels of the Sample Respondents

	Educational Level						
Community	*Illiterate*	*Primary*	*Middle*	*High*	*Higher Secondary*	*Graduate and Above*	*Total*
SC	10	7	1	8		2	28
	35.7%	25.0%	3.6%	28.6%		7.1%	100.0%
	66.7%	77.8%	33.3%	47.1%		10.0%	35.0%
ST		1		1	1		3
		33.3%		33.3%	33.3%		100.0%
		11.1%		5.9%	6.3%		3.8%
MBC	5	1	2	4	8	6	26
	19.2%	3.8%	7.7%	15.4%	30.8%	23.1%	100.0%
	33.3%	11.1%	66.7%	23.5%	50.0%	30.0%	32.5%
BC				4	7	12	23
				17.4%	30.4%	52.2%	100.0%
				23.5%	43.8%	60.0%	28.8%
Total	15	9	3	17	16	20	80
	18.8%	11.3%	3.8%	21.3%	20.0%	25.0%	100.0%
	100.0%	100.0%	100.0%	100.0%	100.0%	100.0%	100.0%

Source: Primary Data.

Table 1a shows that out of the 80 sample households, 28 (35 per cent) belong to the SC community, 3 households (3.8 per cent) belong to the ST community, 26 households (3.5 per cent) are in the MBC community and 23 households (28.8 per cent) are in the category of BC community.

Community and Occupation

Table 2 presents the community and occupation-wise distribution of the sample respondents.

Table 2
Community and Occupation of the Sample Respondents

Community	*Occupation*					*Total*
	Agricultural Landlord	*Agricultural Labour*	*Business*	*Unskilled Labour*	*Government Employed*	
SC	1	9	3	14	1	28
	3.6%	32.1%	10.7%	50.0%	3.6%	100.0%
	5.3%	47.4%	60.0%	87.5%	4.8%	35.0%
ST		2			1	3
		66.7%			33.3%	100.0%
		10.5%			4.8%	3.8%
MBC	6	8	1	2	9	26
	23.1%	30.8%	3.8%	7.7%	34.6%	100.0%
	31.6%	42.1%	20.0%	12.5%	42.9%	32.5%
BC	12		1		10	23
	52.2%		4.3%		43.5%	100.0%
	63.2%		20.0%		47.6%	28.8%
Total	19	19	5	16	21	80
	23.8%	23.8%	6.3%	20.0%	26.3%	100.0%
	100.0%	100.0%	100.0%	100.0%	100.0%	100.0%

Source: Primary Data.

The table indicates that community-wise, out of the 28 respondents belonging to the SC category, 9 are agricultural labourers and 14 are unskilled labourers, while only one is found in the government sector and engaged as agricultural landlord. Among the 26 respondents in the MBC community, a total of 10 respondents are engaged either as agricultural labourer or as unskilled labourer, while 15 respondents are in the agricultural landlord and government categories. In the case of BC respondents, no one is engaged in the agricultural labour or unskilled labour category, while out of the 23 respondents, as many as 22 respondents are engaged either as agricultural landlord or in the government sector. This once again shows the dominance of the respondents belonging to the BC and MBC communities over the SC respondents in positing themselves in better occupation.

Community and Income Levels

The occupation of the respondents is analysed along with their communities with the help of Table 3.

Table 3 indicates that out of the 28 respondents belonging to the SC community, the average monthly income levels of 26 respondents (92.9 per cent) are less than Rs.1000, which clearly indicates that all these

Table 3
Community and Income Levels of the Sample Respondents

Income Levels (Rs.)	*Community*				*Total*
	SC	*ST*	*MBC*	*BC*	
Upto Rs.1000	26	2	11		39
	66.7%	5.1%	28.2%		100.0%
	92.9%	66.7%	42.3%		48.8%
Rs. 1001-5000	1	1	9	10	21
	4.8%	4.8%	42.9%	47.6%	100.0%
	3.6%	33.3%	34.6%	43.5%	26.3%
More than Rs.5000	1		6	13	20
	5.0%		30.0%	65.0%	100.0%
	3.6%		23.1%	56.5%	25.0%
Total	28	3	26	23	80
	35.0%	3.8%	32.5%	28.8%	100.0%
	100.0%	100.0%	100.0%	100.0%	100.0%

Source: Primary Data.

households are living below the poverty line, as the per day income is just around Rs.33 for the total household. In the case of the 3 respondents belonging to the ST community, 2 respondents are in the lowest income slab, while the other one respondent is in the income class of Rs.1001-5000 per month. In the case of 26 respondents, who are belonging to the MBC community, 11 respondents (42.3 per cent) are in the lowest income group, 9 respondents (34.6 per cent) are in the income group of Rs.1001-5000 and only 6 respondents (23.1 per cent) are in the highest income class of more than Rs.5000 per month. As far as the 23 respondents belonging to the BC community is concerned, there are 10 respondents (43.5 per cent) in the Rs.1001-5000 income class and the remaining 13 respondents (56.5 per cent) are earning more than Rs.5000 per month on an average. This shows the relatively better-off nature of the respondents belonging to the BC community compared to the respondents belonging to other communities.

PROBLEMS OF DROP OUT AMONG THE SAMPLE HOUSEHOLDS

Table 4 presents the sex-wise distribution of dropped out children among the sample respondents.

Table 4
Drop out and Sex

Sex of the Dropped out child			*Total*
Male	*Female*	*Both*	
15	16	9	40
37.5%	40.0%	22.5%	100.0%
100.0%	100.0%	100.0%	100.0%

Source: Primary Data.

The table indicates that out of the 40 households in which dropping out exists, in 15 households (37.5 per cent) male child has dropped out, while in 16 households (40 per cent) female child has dropped out and in the other 9 households (22.5 per cent) children belonging to both the genders have dropped out. This indicates that the problem of dropping out is marginally higher among the female children compared to that of male children.

Community and Drop out

Dropping out of children is influenced the community to which the household belongs, which has been brought out by many empirical studies, as noted earlier in literature review. This happens since some of the communities have more social space to attain their social rights compared to others. This is analysed with the help of primary data collected from the Kanchipuram district. Table 5 presents the details regarding community-wise dropping out among the sample households.

Table 5
Community-wise Drop out among the Sample Respondents

Drop out Levels (Rs.)	*Community*				*Total*
	SC	*ST*	*MBC*	*BC*	
Yes	26 65.0% 92.9%	2 5.0% 66.7%	12 30.0% 46.2%		40 100.0% 50.0%
No	2 5.0% 7.1%	1 2.5% 33.3%	14 35.0% 53.8%	23 57.5% 100.0%	40 100.0% 50.0%
Total	28 35.0% 100.0%	3 3.8% 100.0%	26 32.5% 100.0%	23 28.8% 100.0%	80 100.0% 100.0%

Source: Primary Data.

Out of the 40 sample households in which there is dropping out, as many as 26 households (65 per cent) belong to the SC community, 2 (5 per cent) belong to the ST community and 12 households (30 per cent) belong to the MBC community, while there is no dropping out among the sample households belonging to the BC community. This underscores the fact that dropping out is heavily influenced by the community to which the household belongs, which has been proved by many empirical studies.

Educational Level and Drop out

The educational attainment of the parents is the most important determinant in the extent of dropping out of children. The details regarding educational level of the respondent and dropping out is shown in Table 6.

Table 6
Educational Levels and Drop out among the Sample Respondents

Drop Out	*Educational Level of the Parent*					*Total*
	Illiterate	*Middle*	*High*	*Higher Secondary*	*Graduate and Above*	
Yes	15 37.5% 100.0%	3 7.5% 100.0%	22 55.0% 84.6%			40 100.0% 50.0%
No			4 10.0% 15.4%	16 40.0% 100.0%	20 50.0% 100.0%	40 100.0% 50.0%
Total	15 18.8% 100.0%	3 3.8% 100.0%	26 32.5% 100.0%	16 20.0% 100.0%	20 25.0% 100.0%	80 100.0% 100.0%

Source: Primary Data.

The table suggests that out of the 40 households in which dropping out exists, the heads of 15 households (37.5 per cent) are illiterate, 3 households (7.5 per cent) have middle school level education and the heads of 22 households (55 per cent) have high school level education. Thus, none of them have studied beyond the level of high school. In the case of the other 40 sample households in which there is no dropping out, the minimum educational level of the heads of the households is high school and thus none is illiterate. Out of the 40 households, 16 households (40 per cent) have studies up to the level of higher secondary level and heads of 20 households (50 per cent) are in the class of 'graduate and above'. Hence, when the educational levels of the parents themselves is quite low, there will be dropping out of their children, as borne out by many earlier studies.

Occupation and Drop out

When head of the household is engaged in low-earning occupation, the possibility of the child drop out increases. This is analysed with the help of data presented in Table 7.

The table shows that out of the 40 households in which dropping out exists, the heads of the 19 households (47.5 per cent) are working as agricultural labourers and 16 households (40 per cent) are working as unskilled labourers. The heads of 2 households are engaged as agricultural landlords and in 3 households, the respondents are self-employed in business. In the case of the other 40 households, in which there is no dropping out, as many 21 sample households (52.5 per cent) are engaged in the government sector, while the heads of the 17 households (42.5 per cent) are working as cultivating farmers or agricultural landlords. Thus, the nature of occupation plays an important role in determining the extent of dropping out.

Table 7
Occupation and Drop out among the Sample Respondents

Drop Out	*Occupation*					*Total*
	Agricultural Landlord	*Agricultural Labour*	*Business*	*Unskilled Labour*	*Government Employed*	
Yes	2	19	3	16		40
	5.0%	47.5%	7.5%	40.0%		100.0%
	10.5%	100.0%	60.0%	100.0%		50.0%
No	17		2		21	40
	42.5%		5.0%		52.5%	100.0%
	89.5%		40.0%		100.0%	50.0%
Total	19	19	5	16	21	80
	23.8%	23.8%	6.3%	20.0%	26.3%	100.0%
	100.0%	100.0%	100.0%	100.0%	100.0%	100.0%

Source: Primary Data.

Drop out and Literacy Levels

The educational levels of all the members of a household are analysed here.

Table 8
Mean Years of Education of Children among the Sample Respondents

Sex	*Drop Out*		*Total*
	Yes	*No*	
Male	8.59	12.47	10.26
Female	5.26	10.06	7.66
Total	6.92	11.24	8.93

Source: Computed from primary Data.

In order to compare the literacy levels of the children who have dropped out and those who have not, the mean years of education has been arrived separately for males and females. It indicates that the mean score of educational level of male in the dropped out households is 8.59 years and among the female children it is only 5.26 years. But, in the households where there is no drop out the respective figures are12.47 and 10.06 years, which shows a marked difference among both the genders. Moreover, the mean years of education of the female children where there is no drop out is higher than that of the male children where is drop out. Also, the mean total years of education in the dropped out households is only 6.92, whereas it is 11.24 in the other households.

Reasons for Dropping out

To understand the nature and extent of dropping out among the sample households better, it is pertinent to know the reasons for the same. The sample respondents have been asked to provide at least one reason for the existence of dropping out in their households, which is tabulated in Table 9.

Table 9
Reasons for Dropping out among Sample Respondents

Reasons of Dropping out	*Frequency*	*Percent*	*Cumulative Percent*
School is far away	15	37.5	37.5
Did not Study well	1	2.5	40.0
Low Family Income	24	60.0	100.0
Total	40	100.0	

Source: Primary Data.

Out of the 40 households in which the problem exists, 15 households (37.5 per cent) assert that distance of the school is the determining factor. While there this one government school in every village, the level of educational attainment of the child depends directly on the level of that of school. That is, if that school is a primary level school, many of the children, especially the female children will be forced to cut short their educational career at that level itself. Though, higher level schools will be available in the nearby towns, parents will be reluctant to send their children. Thus, the households say that there should be one school at least up to the high school level in every village. Most of the households feel that their low income level is the reason for their children to drop out. This has happened in 24 households (60 per cent). Thus, as noted earlier, though school education is provided at free of cost, parents opine that there are many hidden cost, which they have to pay, like the expenditure on stationeries, examination fees and others. Moreover, when the school is not nearby, they also have to incur transport charges. Only one household opines that the child did not study well enough to continue his / her study. This indicates the role and responsibility that the State has to play to reduce the problem of dropping out.

SUGGESTIONS

- The government should come forward to set up a school in every village and / or upgrade the levels of the existing schools.
- The existing facilities in the government need to be enhanced enormously in order to retain the students, particularly the female students.
- It is always important to iron the cause of the problem, rather than the consequence. Hence, the major reason for drop out, viz., poor family income should be tackled immediately, to arrest any further increase in drop out.
- The gender phenomenon of drop out, i.e., dropping out of more female children than male children, should be given more attention in order to increase the literacy level of the female children.

- Drop out needs to be plugged immediately as it has led to declining literacy levels among the sample households and particularly among the female children.

CONCLUSION

This study clearly brings out the nature and extent of the problem of drop out among the sample households in the district of Kanchipuram. It is concluded that the nature of occupation, level of income, educational levels of the parents and also the place of residence of the parents play the most significant role in deciding the extent of drop out among the children. Moreover, the distance of the existing school, particularly that of the higher level of school and also the facilities extended at the schools work as impediments or the problems faced by the dropped out children. Hence, the government should come forward to improve the levels of the existing schools and also to reduce the distance of schools by creating more schools in the rural areas.

REFERENCES

Bhatty, Kiran, (1998), "Educational Deprivation in India, A Survey of Field Investigations' *Economic and Political Weekly*, July 4th.

Dube, Leela, (1981), "On the Economic Roles of children in India Methodological Issues" in G. Rodgers and G. Standing (eds.) *Child Work, Poverty and Underdevelopment*, ILO.

Filmer, D., and Lant, Pritchett, (1999), "Educational Enrolment and Attainment in India-Household, Wealth, Gender, Village and State Effects". *Journal of Educational Planning and Administration*, Vol. 3, No. 2.

Jaychandaran, Usha, (2001), "Understanding School Attendance and Children's Work Participation in India", *Journal of Educational Planning and Administration*, Vol. 15, No. 1-4.

Nayar, Usha, (1993), Universal Primary Education of Rural Girls in India NCERT. New Delhi.

Pandey, G.D. and P. P. Talwar, (1980), "Some Correlates of Literacy, Educational Attainment among Children in Rural Areas of UP", *Demography India* (1) and (2).

Ramachandran, Vimala, (2002), Gender and Social Equity. Hierarchies of Access.

The European Commission.

Reddy, Shiva and P. Sanjeeva Reddy, (1992), "Inequality of Educational Opportunity in Rural Areas: A Case Study". *Journal of Educational Planning and Administration*, Vol. VI, No. 3 July.

The Probe Team, (1999), Public Report on Basic Education in India, Oxford University Press.

World Bank Report, (1997), Primary Education in India – Development in Practice, Allied Publishers, New Delhi.

6

EDUCATIONAL ATTAINMENT AND WELFARE INTERVENTIONS FOR THE UNDER-PRIVILEGED IN PONDICHERRY

D. UMA

INTRODUCTION

The govt. of India allocated a sizeable amount of the revenue in the plan periods for the education sector with the due understanding of its importance in human resource development. On the other hand, due to the differential caste system existing in India, the govt. could not bring about equality among the population. The govt. in order to bring about economic equality among the social groups, stated giving preferences and priorities to the underprivileged social group the so called scheduled caste population. The assistance provided to them is on an increase but it has not benefited the total scheduled caste population. Hence by giving preferences and priorities in all the aspects and sectors of the economy, the scheduled caste people's status is enhances. For improving their status the govt. has focused on enhancing their education and health station as this is a way important contributing factor for human capital. Various schemes and assistance in provided for their education and health facilities. This paper analyses the various educational facility provided by the union territory of Pondicherry to the schedule caste people.

Keeping in mind the above problem this paper attempts to give a view of the difference that exist in the educational attainment among the SC population in Pondicherry. The education received by people of this community from the primary to the collegiate level. Various schemes and assistance provided by govt. of Pondicherry for the enhancement of their welfare. The analysis is based on the data available as on 2007.

The schedule caste population in 1,57,771 which is found to be 16.19% of the total population of 9,74,345 of 2001 census. The scheduled caste population is equally scattered among all the form regions contributing to 16% to 18% to the total population.

Table 1
Scheduled Caste population in the U.T. of Pondicherry

Region	*S.C. Population*	*Percentage*
Puducherry	1,20,980	16.45
Karaikal	30,868	18.07
Yanam	5,802	18,48
Mahe	121	0.33
Total	1,57,771	16.19

Source: *www.pon.inc.in*

Pie Diagram

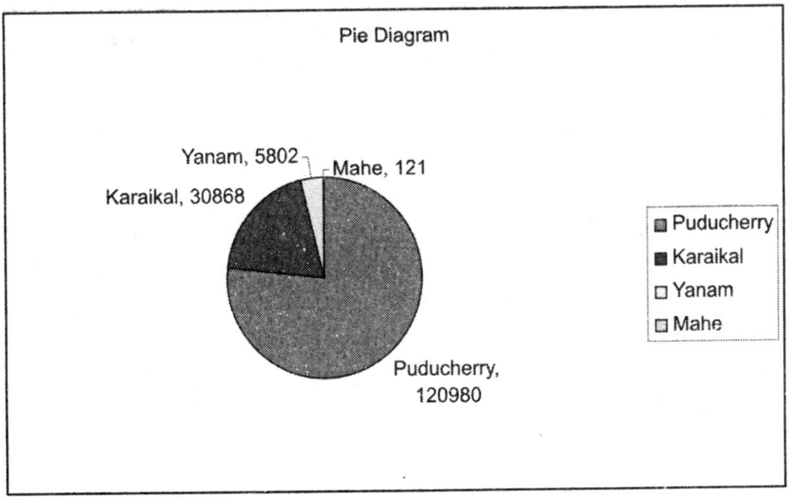

Table 2
Distribution of S.C. population in the Rural and Urban area

Rural/Urban	*Total Population*	*Scheduled Caste*	*Percentage*
Rural	3,25,726	88,545	27,18
Urban	6,48,619	69,226	10.67
Total	9,74,345	1,57,771	16.19

Source: *www.pon.inc.in*

As per the 2001 census the rural and urban distribution of scheduled caste population varies. In the rural area the population is high which amounts for 27.18%, whereas in the urban area it is 10.67%. Hence most of these people still live in rural areas than in urban areas. As per the constitution of Pondicherry, scheduled caste order 1964, the following 16 communities are notified as scheduled castes in the U.T. of Pondicherry.

An Adi Dravidar welfare dept. has been set p in this U.T. of Poly in order to promote and develop the status of S.C. peoples and improve the socio – economic and educational condition of the people living below the poverty line in the U.T. of Pondicherry.

Bar Diagram

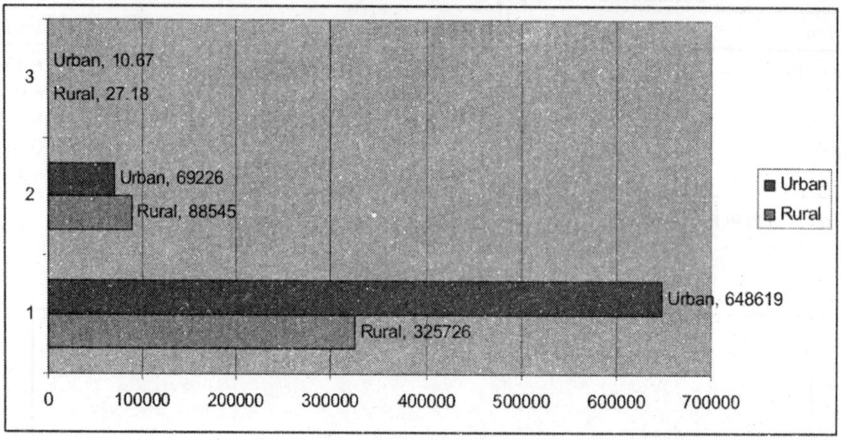

Table 3
Adi Dravida Welfare – Indicators of Socio Economic Development

Sl.No.	*Item*	*Unit*	*As on 31.03.2007*
1.	Purchase, Distribution and Development of House Sites	Nos.	Nil
2.	House Construction subsidy	Nos.	422
3.	Free distribution of Dhoties and Sarees to poor SC	Nos.	156900
4.	Financial Assistance to poor SC brides, Pregnant and lactating Women	Nos.	1351
5.	Free distribution of modern tools and implements	Nos.	Nil
6.	Award to inter-caste married couples	Nos.	29
7.	Construction and maintenance of community halls	Nos.	(Scheme transferred to LAD)
8.	Grant-in-aid to local bodies, water borne latrine for civic amenities to sweepers and scavengers	Works	23
9.	Financial Assistance to SC people to perform funeral rites	Nos.	886

Source: *www.pon.inc.in*

Food, Clothing and Shelter are the various basic amenities required for human being. With this as the centre point there are various schemes provided to the scheduled caste population for socio-economic development. Many people have utilized the assistance provided by the govt.

Facilities have been given for the purchase, distribution and development of house sites. Subsidy is also provided for House Construction. Nearly 422 people have utilized the subsidy given for House construction. Though majority of the population have not made use of the facility, a lesser group have availed the facility, according to 2007 data.

Free Dhoties and sarees were distributed to the poor SC people. Out of the total 1,57,771 SC population 1,56,900 people have received this gift from the govt. which accounts from 99%. The govt. has covered almost all the people in the U.T. of Poly.

Financial Assistance was provided to the brides, Pregnant and lactating women of the Scheduled Caste population 1,351 women were the beneficiaries who took the assistance. As the govt. provides pre-natal and post-natal care for women for safety motherhood. Since it is an important component of health indicator.

To enhance the status of the Scheduled Caste population, the govt. encourages the inter-caste marriages between Scheduled Caste population and other communities. Awards are given to inter caste married couples. 29 couples got the award during the year 2007, for conducting marriage between other communities.

Construction and maintenance of community halls for these people are implemented. Govt. has provided Grant-in-aid to local bodies, for construction of water borne latrine for civic amenities. It is provided to sweepers and scavengers who are still treated as most under privileged people. To perform funeral rites financial assistance is provided to Scheduled Caste people. In the year 2007 886 people have taken the assistance. Aid in provided for the upliftment of the down trodden at all the stages. Thus various welfare schemes are provided for the enhancement of the status of the Scheduled Caste population. Apart form these socio economic welfare measures, the govt. realizing the importance of education for the people has provided various amenities for educating the people. Since education brings sustainable development various land huge amount of assistance is given educate this population.

In the educational areas, various students welfare schemes are implemented from Pre-matric educational incentives to professional college, assistance is provided to the S.C. population. The various schemes are as follows:

Incentives are provided at pre-matric level as basic education is very important. 6957 girl students are given retention scholarship as girls are

Table 4
Pre-matric Educational Incentives

Sl.No.	*Pre-Matric Educational Incentives*	*Unit*	*Indicators as on 31.03.2007*
1.	Retention Scholarship to SC girl students	Nos.	6957
2.	Stipend to ITI Trainees	Nos.	161
3.	Stipend to VTC Trainees	Nos.	93
4.	Pre-matric scholarship	Nos.	12851
5.	Opportunity Cost	Nos.	7671

Source: *www.pon.inc.in*

the vulnerable group who has to be encouraged. Pre-matric scholarship are give to 12851 students, they have availed this benefit. Stipends are provided for students tubing training. 161 students and 93 students have got the assistance for ITI training and VTC training, respectively. Opportunity cost benefit is provided for 7671 students for pursuing their studies forgoing their incomes. Hence to give basic foundation in education the govt. provides various financial incentives. Apart from the financial incentive, material incentives are also provided to them for continuing their education.

The basic amenities like uniforms, text books and stationery are provided to the students of Primary classes. Students who have taken the hostel facilities, the inmates are provided by uniforms. 2382 students were given their school uniforms, as a token of encouragement. Special incentives were given to 175 students. Apart from the pre-matric incentives and scholarships, for students who pursue their higher studies post-matric scholarships are given. 6670 students got the post matric scholarships.

From the comparison of the table 5 and 6 it can be noted that when students come to post matric higher education level from pre matric level the number dwindles to almost 50%. The takers of post-matric scholarship is almost half the number. To encourage higher education the govt. gives "Dr. Ambedkar Memorial Award" to the best students. Six students have got the Award in the year 2007, which is an appreciable deed.

Table 5
Incentives

Sl.No.	*Incentives*	*Unit*	*Indicators as on 31.03.2007*
1.	Distribution of uniforms, text books and stationery to the students of Primary Classes	Nos.	N.A.
2.	Distribution of uniforms to inmates of hostels	Nos.	2382
3.	Special incentives to SC students	Nos.	175
4.	Dr. Ambedkar Memorial Award	Nos.	6
5.	Post-Matric Scholarships	Nos.	6670
6.	Supplemental Maintenance Allowance	Nos.	Nil

Source: *www.pon.inc.in*

Scholarships are awarded to Scheduled Caste students who are pursuing elementary and secondary level of education continuously without hardship. For native residence of the U.T. of Pondicherry, if the parental annual income is less than 24,000/- the student is gives Rs.1,500/- per annum from VI std to VIII std. When the student pursues to higher class they are eli-gible to get Rs.25,000/- per annum from IX std. to X std.

Table 6

Award of Pre-Matric scholarship to S.C. students

1.	Name of the Act/Rules	Award of Pre-matric scholarship to S.C. students
2.	Objective	Award of Scholarship to scheduled caste students who are pursing elementary and secondary level of education continuously without hardship.
3.	Brief write-up of the scheme	i) Rs.1,500/- per annum per student from VI std. to VIII std. ii) Rs.2,500/- per annum per student from IX & X std.
4.	Eligibility	a) Annual income of the parent/guardian shall not exceed Rs.24,000- b) Nativity/residence in this U.T. for not less than 5 years
5.	Enclosures with Application	a) Proof of identity b) Caste/Income/Residence-cum-nativity certificate issued by the competent authority

Source: *www.pon.inc.in*

Table 7

Award of Opportunity Cost of Parents to S.C. Girl Students

1.	Name of the Act/Rules	Award of opportunity cost parents of S.C. girl students
2.	Objective	To financially assist the SC parents for sending school their daughters who otherwise earn livelihood for the family engaging themselves in menial labour.
3.	Brief write-up of the scheme	Rs.3,000/- per academic year payable to the SC parent for each daughters studying in classes VI to XII standard.
4.	Eligibility	(a) Annual income of the parents shall not be more than Rs.24,000/- (b) For girl students only. (c) Student should have been promoted to next higher class.
5.	Enclosures with Application	a) Proof of identity b) Caste/Income/Residence-cum-nativity certificate issued by the competent authority

Source: *www.pon.inc.in*

For the native of U.T, who parents annual income does not exceed more than 24,000/- assistance is provided. This assistance is only for girl students, who have been promoted to next higher class. Rs.3,000/- per academic year is provided to the parents for each daughters studying in classes VI to XII std. This financial assistance is provided to the parents for sending to school their daughters who otherwise would have earned a livelihood for the family by engaging themselves in menial labour. Hence the opportunity cost assistance is for the income foregone by going to school for getting educated.

Students who have obtained above 75% marks in Higher Secondary Course examination and studying in professional colleges, reimbursement

Table 8
Reimbursement of College Fees to Deserving SC Students Studying in Professional College

1	Name of the Act/Rules	Reimbursement of college fees to deserving Schedules Caste Students studying in Professional colleges.
2	Objective	The scheme is to reimburse the tuition fees and examination fess paid by poor Scheduled Caste Students who have obtained Marks above 75% in Higher Secondary Course Examination and studying in Govt/Govt. recognized private Professional colleges.
3	Brief write-up of the scheme	The scheme provides to the reimbursement of tuition fees and examination fees paid by poor S.C. students who have obtained 75% marks and above in Higher Secondary Course Examination and studying in Govt./Govt. recognized private Professional Colleges with view to minimize their financial hardship.
4	Eligibility	a) Annual Income of parent – No limitb) Find place in 'Top 20 Rank' in the HSC marks and selected through 'CENTAC' for admission in professional colleges.
5	Enclosures with Application	a) Caste/Residence Certificate issued by the Revenue Department b) Certificate of Head of Institution c) Original fee Receipt; d) Attested copy of HSC mark list

Source: *www.pon.inc.in*

is given. The annual income of parent has no limit and if they find a place in 'Top 20 Rank' in the HSC marks and selected through 'CENTAC' for admission in professional colleges, their tuition fees and examination fees are reimbursed, with a view to minimize their financial hardship to encourage them to continue their studies such facilities are given.

Apart from various incentives and financial assistance the govt. has also built hostels for the students' facility. There are 18 hostels for Boys and 10 hostels for the girl students. 1567 boys and 815 girl students have availed the hostel facilities. The hostels are well equipped and provide all basic amenities to the students.

Table 9
Hostel Facilities for the SC Students

Sl. No.	*Item*	*Unit*	*Indicators as on 31.03.2007*
1.	Hostels	-	-
	1. Boys	Nos.	18
	2. Girls	Nos.	10
2.	Students Strength in Hostels	-	-
	1. Boys	Nos.	1567
	2. Girls	Nos.	815

Source: *www.pon.inc.in*

In spite of giving all facilities and amenities to impart education and promote the underprivileged people, the Scheduled Caste population, the enrollment of students in college level and school level is not very significant. From the statistics of 2007-2008 it is evident that only 15% to 20% of Scheduled Caste students are enrolled at both college and school levels.

CONCLUSION

On the whole the students enrollment in the U.T in 44,143 which amounts for 28%. The strength of girls students are equal to the boy students, 21,866 and 22,277 respectively. People have realized the importance of educating girl children. The incentives given by the govt. has played a vital role in the education of girl children.

Relining the situation, the govt. of Pondicherry has taken initiative to give huge amount of assistance and incentives for removing the disparity among the people. This assistance and incentives have encouraged nearly 20 to 30% of the population. In the process of economic development, the efforts of the govt., along with time factor will definitely bring down the socio-economic disparity in the society.

REFERENCES

Bajpai, Nirupam, Ravindra Dholakia and Jeffrey D. Sachs. (2008), 'Scaling up Primary Education Services in Rural India: Case Studies of Andhra Pradesh and Karnataka', Center on Globalization and Sustainable Development, Columbia University, Working Paper No. 34, New York.

Banerji, Rukmini (2003), 'Making the Grade: Teach Children the Joy of Learning.' Times of India, July 14, New Delhi.

Planning Commission (2006a), Towards Faster and More Inclusive Growth – An Approach to the 11th Five Year Plan, Govt. of India, June 14. (Referred to as "Approach Paper to 11th Plan"). (*http://planningcommission.nic.in*)

Ramachandran, Vimla, (2005), Why School Teachers are Demotivated and Disheartened, Economic and Political Weekly, May 21-27.

State Report Card (2006), National University of Educational Planning and Administration. (*www.depemis.org*).

Tamil Nadu Human Development Report (2003): Government of Tamil Nadu. (*http://www.tn.gov.in*) (*www.govermentof Pondicherry.in*).

7

OBSTACLES TO SCHOOL LIFE EXPECTANCY

J. MAHESWARI

INTRODUCTION

Human capital is an extensive and versatile conception encompassing different types of investment in people. Education, Health and nutrition are indisputably significant aspect of such investment, particularly in developing countries where deficiencies in these respects may severely limit the population's ability to engage in productive activities.

The skills and knowledge embodied in an individual can be defined as human capital. All individuals attain a certain stock of human capital and this level is primarily influenced by education and training. Blaug, (1972) summarizes the link between education and earnings by stating that "the simplest explanation of the universal association between education and earnings across sectors, industries and occupational categories around the world is that the better educated are generally more flexible and more motivated, adapt themselves more easily to changing circumstances, benefit more from work experience and training, act with greater initiative in problem-solving situations, assume supervisory responsibility more quickly and, in short, are more productive than the less educated, even when their education has taught them no specific skills."

The knowledge economy of the coming decades will require increasing number of people with unique knowledge and intellectual skills • While India with its billion plus population and demographically endowed with abundant younger generation have ample of opportunity in the knowledge era.

The overall educational attainment achieved during the past few decades has placed India in the 174th place out of 205 world countries in terms of literacy level.

India suffers from acute economic and social disparities. This article addresses four dimensions of such disparities, from the educational profile of India *viz*. regional, rural-urban, social, and gender. Hence the objective of this paper is to measure

Country	*Literacy Rate 2005 %*
Uk	99.9
Russia	99.4
US	97.0
Israel	96.9
Singapore	92.5
China	90.9
Mexico	90.3
South Africa	82.4
Iran	77.0
India	61.0
Bangladesh	41.1

- Regional variation in educational attainments
- Gender discrimination in educational attainments
- Child labour and its impact on educational attainments
- Social disparity resulting in discrimination in educational attainment

One of the Millennium Development Goals (MDGs) agreed in September 2000 at a UN summit of world leaders is the achievement of universal primary school attendance for boys and girls. This, of course, requires a 100% primary school completion rate, that is, that

- All students entering grade 1 are retained until grade 5.
- A complete closing of the gender gap in educational attainments.
- Concluding social exclusion in educational stream

The MDG implied in these terms reflects recognition of the importance of basic (primary/elementary) education. This is particularly pertinent in India where primary education has historically been neglected by the state, with educational expenditures being concentrated on the tertiary sector. Though, the situation has started to change lately as major chunk of educational budget is now directed towards elementary education.

There are vast inequalities in educational attainment in India and striking diversity in educational indicators across its states.

On the basis of literacy rate, State/UTs can be grouped as under:

- *High Literacy Rate (80% and above)* - Kerala (90.86%), Mizoram (88.80%), Lakshadweep (86.66%), Goa (82.01%),Chandigarh (81.94%),Delhi (81.67%), A & N Islands (81.30%) and Pondicherry (81.24%).
- *Literacy Rate above National Average (64.8%) and below 80%* - Daman & Diu (78.18%), Maharashtra (76.88%), Himachal Pradesh (76.48%), Tamil Nadu (73.45%), Tripura (73.19%), Uttaranchal (71.62%), Manipur (70.53%), Punjab (69.65%), Gujarat (69.14%),

Sikkim (68.81%), West Bengal (68.64%), Haryana (67.91%), Karnataka (66.64%) and Nagaland (66.59%).

- *Literacy Rate below National Average* (64.8%) – Chhattisgarh (64.66%), Madhya Pradesh (63.74%), Assam (63.25%), Orissa (63.08%), Meghalaya (62.56%), Andhra Pradesh (60.47%), Rajasthan (60.41%), Dadra & Nagar Haveli (57.63%), Uttar Pradesh (56.27%), Jammu & Kashmir (55.52%), Arunachal Pradesh (54.34%), Jharkhand (53.56%) and Bihar 47.00

Regional Variation in Education

Rank	*State/UTs*	*Literacy Rate*	*Male Literacy Rate*	*Female Literacy Rate*
1.	Kerala	90.86	94.24	87.72
2.	Mizoram	88.80	92.53	86.75
3.	Lakshadweep	86.66	90.72	80.47
4.	Goa	82.01	88.62	76.47
5.	Chandigarh	81.94	88.42	75.37
6.	Delhi	81.67	87.33	75.24
7.	Andaman & Nicobar Islands	81.30	86.76	74.71
8.	Puducherry	81.24	86.33	73.90
9.	Daman & Diu	78.18	86.14	67.42
10.	Maharashtra	76.88	85.97	67.03
11.	Himachal Pradesh	76.48	85.35	65.61
12.	Tamilnadu	73.45	83.28	64.91
13.	Tripura	73.19	82.42	64.33
14.	Uttarakhand	71.62	81.02	63.36
15.	Manipur[1]	70.53	80.33	61.46
16.	Punjab	69.65	79.66	60.53
17.	Gujarat	69.14	78.49	60.40
18.	Sikkim	68.81	77.38	59.63
19.	West Bengal	68.64	77.02	59.61
20.	Haryana	67.91	76.10	59.61
21.	Karnataka	66.64	76.06	57.80
22.	Nagaland	66.59	76.04	56.87
23.	Chhattisgarh	64.66	75.70	55.73
24.	Madhya Pradesh	63.74	75.35	54.61
25.	Assam	63.25	75.23	51.85
26.	Orissa	63.08	71.28	50.51
27.	Meghalaya	62.56	71.18	50.43
28.	Andhra Pradesh	60.47	71.16	50.29
29.	Rajasthan	60.41	70.32	43.85
30.	Dadra & Nagar Haveli	57.63	68.82	43.53
31.	Uttar Pradesh	56.27	67.30	43.00
32.	Jammu & Kashmir	55.52	66.60	42.22
33.	Arunachal Pradesh	54.34	65.43	40.23
34.	Jharkhand	53.56	63.83	38.87
35.	Bihar	47.00	59.68	33.12

Source: Census 2001

Rural-Urban Gap (Literates) - Census 2001 (In millions)

	Total NAR (%)	*Male NAR (%)*	*Female NAR(%)*	*Difference Male-Female*	*GPI Female/Male*
Urban	76.8	77.3	76.2	1.1	0.99
Rural	70.7	74.7	66.5	8.2	0.89
Richest 20%	81.9	81.8	81.9	-0.1	1.00
Poorest 20%	64.0	67.7	60.2	7.5	0.89
Total	72.1	75.3	68.7	6.6	0.91

	Persons	*Male*	*Female*
All Areas	560.68 (64.8%)	336.53 (75.3%)	224.15 (53.7%)
Rural Areas	361.87 (58.7%)	223.55 (70.7%)	138.32 (46.1%)
Urban Areas	199.81 (79.9%)	113.98 (86.3%)	85.83 (72.9%)
SC	75.31 (54.69%)	47.43 (66.64%)	27.88 (41.90%)
ST	32.38 (47.10%)	20.56 (59.17%)	11.82 (34.76%)

GPI: gender parity index. - Data source: India 2000 MICS.

Over half of the working children (54%) are in agriculture, and most others are employed either in construction (15.5%) or in household work (18%). About 5% are in manufacturing jobs, and the remainder (about 8%) are scattered across other forms of employment. The table below provides a gender-wise breakup of working children, and their schooling status. Please note that the data are for children in the age group 5-14 years.

Development alone cannot bring peace, prosperity and progress unless social justice and gender equality are ensured. It has been realized that development programs have bypassed women who constitute about half of the population of the country. Findings of various researches on status of women education elucidate that patriarchal society like India confers very meagre importance to their education.

- Gender based inequality.
- Social discrimination and economic exploitation.
- Occupation of girl child in domestic chores.
- Low enrolment of girls in schools.
- Low retention rate and high dropout rate.
- Early marriage,

Added to this the presence of exclusively male teachers, distance to schools (especially in rural India), unhealthy sanitation, absence of midday meals and acute poverty were diagnosed as potential factors of a very high drop out rate for the girl child.

Early marriage inevitably denies children of school age their right to the education they need for their personal development, their preparation for adulthood, and their effective contribution to the future wellbeing of

Sex Wise Literacy Rate From 1971–001 % Age

Year	*Literate*	*Male*	*Female*	*Literacy Gap*
1971	34.45.	5.96 m	21.98	23.98
1981	43.57	56.37	29.75	26.62
1991 2001	52.21 65.38	64.13 75.85	39.29 54.16.	24.84 21.69

Source: Human Development in south Asia 2007

their family and society. Indeed, married girls who would like to continue schooling may be both practically and legally excluded from doing so. The interaction between the number of years of a girl's schooling and the postponement of marriage is firmly established by demographic and fertility studies.

India is the home of 16% of World's total population accommodated in an area of 2.42% of the World's total land area and spends 3.8% of its GNP on education. Socially backward sections, especially scheduled castes and tribes (SCs and STs) have gained little from the new prosperity which rewards disproportionately those with assets, skills and higher education. STs have often been victims of development as a result of displacement. The gender gap in social and economic status, traditionally more in India as compared to other societies; has further widened by the economic reforms and globalization.

Table 1

Gross Enrolment by Stages of all Categories of Students (in millions)

Year	*Primary (I-V)*			*Upper Primary (VI-VIII)*			*High/Hr. Sec./Inter/ Pre-Degree (IX-XII)*		
	Boys	*Girls*	*Total*	*Boys*	*Girls*	*Total*	*Boys*	*Girls*	*Total*
1950-51	13.8	5.4	19.2	2.6	0.5	3.1	1.3	0.2	1.5
1955-56	17.1	7.5	24.6	3.8	1.0	4.8	2.2	0.4	2.6
1960-61	23.6	11.4	35.0	5.1	1.6	6.7	2.7	0.7	3.4
1970-71	35.7	21.3	57.0	9.4	3.9	13.3	5.7	1.9	7.6
1980-81	45.3	28.5	73.8	13.9	6.8	20.7	7.6	3.4	11.0
1990-91	57.0	40.4	97.4	21.5	12.5	34.0	12.8	6.3	19.1
1991-92	58.6	42.3	100.9	22.0	13.6	35.6	13.5	6.9	20.4
1992-93	57.9	41.7	99.6	21.2	12.9	34.1	13.6	6.9	20.5
1993-94	55.1	41.9	97.0	20.6	13.5	34.1	13.2	7.5	20.7
1994-95	60.0	45.1	105.1	22.1	14.3	36.4	14.2	7.9	22.1
1995-96	60.9	46.2	107.1	22.7	14.8	37.5	14.6	8.3	22.9
1996-97	61.4	46.8	108.2	22.9	15.2	38.1	15.3	8.7	24.0
1997-98	62.3	48.0	110.3	23.6	15.9	39.5	16.1	9.3	25.4
1998-99	62.7	49.0	111.7	23.9	16.5	40.4	16.6	10.1	26.7
1999-00	64.1	49.5	113.6	25.1	17.0	42.1	17.2	11.0	28.2
2000-2001	64.0	49.8	11.38	25.3	17.5	42.8	18.9	10.7	27.6
2001-2002	63.6	50.3	11.39	26.1	18.7	44.8	18.4	12.1	30.5
2002-2003	65.1	57.3	12.24	26.3	20.6	46.9	19.5	13.7	33.2
2003-2004	68.4	59.9	12.83	27.2	21.5	48.7	20.6	14.4	35.0

Ministry of Human Resource Development, Department of Education, Annual Reports, New Delhi, India.

Table 2
Cohort Survival Rate

Survival Rate Final Grade	*1999*	*2000*	*2001*	*2002*	*2003*	*2004*
Survival rate final grade (male & Female)	62	59	61	81	79	73
Survival rate final grade (Female only)	60	59	64	76	73	-
Survival rate final grade (Male only)	63	59	60	81	73	-
Retention Rate	89	87	89	87	85	85

Highlights of 2001 Census Literacy Rate State/UT Wise

Table 3
Sex Ratio of Different States of India

State	*Sex Ratio 0-6 Years*
India	927
Andaman &Nicobar Islands	965
Andhra Pradesh	964
Arunachal Pradesh	961
Assam	964
Bihar	938
Chandigarh	845
Chhattisgarh	975
Dadra &Nagar Haveli	973
Daman & Diu	925
Delhi	865
Goa	933
Gujarat	878
Haryana	820
Himachal Pradesh	897
Jammu & Kashmir	927
Jharkhand	966
Karnataka	949
Kerala	963
Lakshadweep	974
Madhya Pradesh	929
Maharashtra	917
Manipur	961
Meghalaya	975
Mizoram	971
Nagaland	975
Orissa	950
Pondicherry	958
Punjab	793
Rajasthan	909
Sikkim	986
Tamil Nadu	939
Tripura	975
Uttar Pradesh	916
Uttaranchal	906
West Bengal	963

Index of Son Preference for Major States in India

States	*Index of Son Preference*	*Rank*
Andhra Pradesh	13.8	11
Bihar	24.5	4
Gujarat	23	6
Haryana	14.3	10
Karnataka	20	8
Kerala	11.7	12
Madhya Pradesh	27.1	2
Maharashtra	18	9
Orissa	23.4	5
Punjab	20.3	7
Rajasthan	25	3
Tamil Nadu	9.2	13
Uttar Pradesh	21.6	1
West Bengal	14.3	10
All India	20	

Source: The Third All India Survey of Family Planning Practices in India

Across India, child labour is accepted as the single largest source of child abuse and exploitation. According to ILO estimates, one-fourth of the working children in the world are Indians. Child labour exists and thrives in all parts of the country, mainly due to interplay between factors constituting the demand and supply of this kind of labour. Child labour thrives in situations where adults are unemployed, families are large, there is a lack of land and other resources, and there is overall backwardness in terms of literacy and skills.

Moreover, since a child needs to be paid only half the wages of an adult, many employers prefer to employ child labour. The stipulation that children are supposed to work for only half the time as adults is invariably not followed. As a result, the child labourer ends up displacing an adult from the work force. This just perpetuates the vicious circle of unemployment, poverty and exploitation for the poor.

The calculated value of the index not only provides the gender disparity in literacy rate for the concerning state (or district) but also make it possible to compare the disparity across various states and also for a state over a period of time because value of the index is obtained by multiplying the gender gap in literacy rate the state i by the standardized

Social group	*Average MPCE 55TH Round*			*Average MPCE 61ST ROUND*		
	Rural	*Urban*	*All*	*Rural*	*Urban*	*All*
ST	386.69	608.79	417.42	426.19	857.46	463.15
SC	418.51	690.52	454.85	474.72	758.38	532.07
OBC	473.65	734.82	529.50	556.72	870.93	635.89
Others	577.22	1004.75	729.45	685.31	1306.10	919.09
All	854.70	854.70	578.62	558.78	1052.36	683.75

value i.e; the ratio of the literacy rate of the country to literacy rate of the state *i*.

The values of the index of gender disparity for various states of the country are given in Table. It can be seen from the table that the value of gender disparity found to be more than 40 in two states namely Rajasthan and Bihar in 1991. In Rajasthan it has reduced from 46.79 in 1991 to 27.48 in 2001. In Bihar it has reduced from 40.92 to 29.38 during the same period. Though, the gender gap in literacy rate is relatively higher in Rajasthan than in Bihar in 2001 but the value of the index of gender disparity is higher (29.38) for Bihar than that (27.48) for the Rajasthan. In fact, proposed index of disparity also take into account of the overall literacy rate of the respective state (or district). In 2001, over all literacy rate of Bihar was very much lower (47.53%) than that (61.03%) for the Rajasthan. Table also shows that, in 1991, 5 states / UTs (Chandigarh, Mijoram, Meghalya, Kerala and Andman & Nikobar) had values of gender disparity less than 10. In 2001 all have shown decline in the gender disparity. Also, in 2001 Punjab, Delhi.

State Wise Index of Gender Disparity

India/States Union/ Territories	Literacy Rate 1991 Total	Males	Females	Index of Gender Disparity	2001 Total	Males	Females	Index of Gender Disparity
Jammu & Kashmir	N.A	N.A	N.A		54.46	65.75	41.82	22.94
Himachal Pradesh	63.94	75.41	52.26	18.90	77.13	86.02	68.08	12.14
Punjab	58.51	65.66	50.41	13.61	69.95	75.63	63.55	9.02
Chandigarh	77.81	82.04	72.34	6.51	81.76	85.65	76.65	5.75
Uttaranchal	57.75	72.79	41.63	28.17	72.28	84.01	60.26	17.16
Haryana	55.85	69.1	40.47	26.76	68.59	79.25	56.31	17.46
Delhi	75.29	82.01	66.99	10.42	81.82	87.37	75	7.89
Rajasthan	38.55	54.99	20.44	46.79	61.03	76.46	44.34	27.48
Uttar Pradesh	40.71	54.82	24.37	39.05	57.36	70.23	42.98	24.80
Bihar	37.49	51.37	21.99	40.92	47.53	60.32	33.57	29.38
Sikkim	56.94	65.7	46.76	17.37	69.68	76.73	61.46	11.44
Arunachal Pradesh	41.59	51.45	29.69	27.32	54.74	64.07	44.24	18.91
Nagaland	61.65	67.62	54.75	10.90	67.11	71.77	61.92	7.66
Manipur	59.89	71.63	47.6	20.95	68.87	77.87	59.7	13.77
Mizoram	82.27	85.61	78.6	4.45	88.49	90.69	86.13	2.69
Tripura	60.44	70.58	49.65	18.08	73.66	81.47	65.41	11.38
Meghalaya	49.1	53.12	44.85	8.79	63.31	66.14	60.41	4.73
Assam	52.89	61.87	43.03	18.60	64.28	71.93	56.03	12.91

(Table Continued)

	Literacy Rate							
	1991				*2001*			
India/States Union/ Territories	*Total*	*Males*	*Females*	*Index of Gender Disparity*	*Total*	*Males*	*Females*	*Index of Gender Disparity*
West Bengal	57.7	67.81	46.56	19.23	69.22	77.58	60.22	13.09
Jharkhand	41.39	55.8	25.52	38.20	54.13	67.94	39.38	27.55
Orissa	49.09	63.09	34.68	30.22	63.61	75.95	50.97	20.50
Chhattisgarh	42.91	58.07	27.52	37.17	65.18	77.86	52.4	20.39
Madhya Pradesh	44.67	58.54	29.35	34.12	64.11	76.8	50.28	21.60
Gujarat	61.57	73.39	48.92	20.75	69.97	80.5	58.6	16.34
Daman & Diu	71.2	82.66	59.4	17.06	81.09	88.4	70.37	11.61
Dadra & Nagar Haveli	40.71	53.56	26.98	34.09	60.03	73.32	42.99	26.38
Maharashtra	64.87	76.56	52.32	19.51	77.27	86.27	67.51	12.68
Andhra Pradesh	44.09	55.13	32.72	26.54	61.11	70.85	51.17	16.81
Karnataka	56.04	67.26	44.34	21.35	67.04	76.29	57.45	14.67
Goa	75.51	83.64	67.09	11.44	82.32	88.88	75.51	8.48
Lakshadweep	81.78	90.18	72.89	11.04	87.52	93.15	81.56	6.91
Kerala	89.81	93.62	86.17	4.33	90.92	94.2	87.86	3.64
Tamil Nadu	62.66	73.75	51.33	18.68	73.47	82.33	64.55	12.64
Pondicherry	74.74	83.68	65.63	12.61	81.49	88.89	74.13	9.46
Andaman & Nicobar	73.02	78.99	65.46	9.67	81.18	86.07	75.29	6.93

Census of India 2001. "Provisional Population Totals, Series 1, Paper 1 of 2001", Registrar General & Census Commissioner of India.

Nagaland, Goa, Lakshadweep and Pondicherry added to this category i.e; gender disparity less than 10. State-wise values of the index of disparity indicate that in all the states and UTs gender gap in literacy rate has narrowed down.

REFERENCES

Census of India, 1991.

Census of India, 2001.

Human Development in South Asia, 2007.

Annual Reports, Department of Education, Ministry of Human Resources Development, Govt. of India.

The Third All-India Survey of Family Planning Practices in India.

8

GENDER DISPARITY IN EDUCATION-EXTENT AND FACTORS – INDIA

S. RAJA RAJAN

INTRODUCTION

The education commission (1964-66) accorded great emphasis on the equity aspect of growth of education. The commission suggested some measures for reducing the disparities nod these suggested measures have been endorsed in the national policy on education (1968). Further the national Policy on Education (1986), its Programme of Action (POA) as well as its modified version of 1992, have shown great concern and given commitment for education for equality. It lays special emphasis on the removal of disparities and suggests measures for equalization of educational opportunities. The policy document assured that the objective of equalization of educational opportunities will be achieved by attending to special needs of backward sections of population that have been denied such as educational opportunities so far. The part IV of the national policy on education (1986) clearly promised equality in education with respect to women scheduled castes, scheduled tribes, minorities and handicapped (Zaidi).

The goal of Universalisation of elementary education (UEE) cannot be achieved if any kind of disparities persist in the system of education. In order to realize the goal of equity in education it is important to address the problem of gender inequities and social equities at different level of educational system. Inequalities in all areas of education remain. Girls, poor and rural children from marginalized regions are least likely to receive education (Education for All).

MILLENNIUM DEVELOPMENT GOALS (MDG) AND GENDER EQUALITY

Gender equality is one of the fundamental goals in human development highlighted at numerous global conferences including the world conference on women in Beijing, the World summit on children, and the Jomtien and Dakar education fora. The importance of gender equality is reaffirmed in the UN Millennium Development Goals.

COMMITMENTS TO GENDER EQUALITY IN EDUCATION

Three out of Six Education for All goals during the World Education Forum in Dakar, Senegal in April 2000 were concerned with gender equality in education.

Goal 2: Ensuring that by 2015 all children, *particularly girls* ... have access to and complete free and compulsory primary education of good quality.

Goal 4: Achieving a 50 per cent improvement in levels of adult literacy by 2015, especially for women.

Goal 5: Eliminating *gender disparities* in primary and secondary education by 2005, and achieving *gender equality* in education by 2015, with a focus on ensuring girl's full and equal access to achievement in basic education of good quality.

The MDG's re-affirmed the concerns of gender equality in two of their objectives:

Goal 2: Ensure that, by 2015, children everywhere, boys and *girls* alike, will be able to complete a full course of primary schooling.

Goal 3: Eliminate *Gender disparity* in primary and secondary education preferably by 2005 and in all levels of education no later than 2015.

Considering Disparities

- Which children are not in school/ learning centres?
- What inhibits their full participation?
- Who should be targeted as a priority?
- How can we improve quality and equality?

FACTORS AFFECTING DISPARITY IN EDUCATION

In order to analyze disparity in access to education at national level, to identify the factors hindering girls disparity in education. These are two major factors:

(a) Demand side (socio-economic, cultural factors which affect the behavior and the choices of parents and students) factors; (b) Supply side (political institutional factors and factors linked to the school) factors.

Demand Side Factors

(i) Socio-Economic Factors are

- Poverty
- Direct costs (fees, uniforms, transportation
- High opportunity costs/lower rate of return
- Girls needed for household/agricultural tasks
- Residence in remote, low population areas
- Limited employment opportunities for graduates
- Lower remuneration for women

(ii) Cultural Factors which Affect the Behavior and The Choices of Parents and Students

- Parents' low level of education
- Lower priority for girls' education
- Girls' education perceived as incompatible with traditional beliefs and/or religious principles
- Early marriages and pregnancies
- Role of the girl/woman as a wife and mother
- Sceptical attitudes towards the benefits and outcomes from educating girls with farming cycle

Supply Side Factors

(i) Political and Institutional Factors such as

- Budget constraints; Structural adjustment programmes
- Insufficient public support for the poor
- Political instability; Inconsistent educational policies
- Poor quality of education programmes
- Ill-adaptation of education systems to local learning needs
- Lack of clear strategy for women and girls' education
- Lack of public support for women in scientific activities
- Limited employment prospects
- Poor data collection mechanisms; inadequate elements for progress assessment and policy formulation

(ii) Factors Linked to the Schools Like

- Limited school/classroom space
- High school fees
- Low proportion of female teachers
- Teachers untrained/not sensitized to gender issues
- Stereotypes at school (curricula, textbooks)
- School curricula in conflict with traditional culture
- Orientation of girls/women to non scientific fields
- Lack of accommodations for or exclusion of pregnant adolescents and young mothers
- Sexual harassment; insecurity
- Distance from school
- Lack of school canteens
- Poor quality of hygienic facilities
- School calendar incompatible with farming cycles

One should also not forget that, due to the structure of the population, where women outnumber men, especially among older generations, equality does not necessarily coincide with 50%. For this reason it is appropriate, when measuring disparity, to provide also a comparison of rates by gender.

ISSUES IN GIRLS EDUCATION AT INTERNATIONAL AND NATIONAL LEVEL

According to Lewis and Lockheed, while girls are catching up to and even surpassing boys in schools in many countries, girls from excluded minority groups remain at the bottom in terms of education. The number of out-of-school girls worldwide has fallen from 60 million in 2006, but the problem persists in countries where minorities are economically, and socially disadvantaged and women are secluded. Most out – of –school girls live in Africa (47 per cent) and South Asia (25 per cent), but in Latin America girls from minority groups represent the highest proportion of out-of-school.

India has made extraordinary progress in enrolment. In 2002 an estimated 25 million children (13 per cent of the age cohort) were out-of-school (World Bank, 2004). By 2005 this number had been roughly halved, with only about 13.5 million children aged 6-13 (less than 7 per cent of the cohort) out-of-school (Social and Rural Research Institute, 2005). The age-specific enrolment in primary education is nearly 94 per cent. Another household study conducted by civic action groups finds similar enrolment rates (Annual Status of Education Report).

About 8 per cent of girls and rural children are not enrolled in school. These figures are higher than those for boys (6 per cent) and for children from urban areas (4 per cent). About two-thirds of those children have never attended school and a third of them have dropped out. About half of all out-of-school children are physically or mentally challenged. Those out of school include 38 per cent of children with disabilities, 10 per cent of Muslim children, 10 per cent of children from scheduled tribes and 8 per cent of children from scheduled castes.

BENEFITS OF GIRLS EDUCATION

In India Human development performance has suffered especially from discrimination against women. The choice of focusing on gender disparity in education is based on the broad social benefits educating girls, which are almost universally acknowledged. They include the following; the more educated mother have low infant and child mortality; children of more educated mothers tend to be better nourished and suffer lies from illness(Thomas, 1990, Schultz, 1993): children (and particularly daughter) of more- educated mothers are more likely to be educated: more years of education women have, later they tend to marry and the fewer children they tend to have; educated women are less likely to die in childbirth; the more educate a women is, the more she is to have opportunities and life choices and avoid being appraised and exploited by her family or social situation; educated women are more likely to be receptive, to participate, to in and influence development initiatives; educated women are more likely to play a role in political and economic decision making at community, regional and national level (UNICEF,1999), King and Hill,1993). A study of Zambia finds that AIDS spread twice as fast among uneducated girls compared to educated girls (Vandermoortele and Delamonica, 2000). In this contest the present study is analysis gender disparity at lower level of education (Primary, middle and sec/ higher secondary) in India.

OBJECTIVES

The objectives of the present study are:

(i) The disparity in enrolment rate for all categories at primary, middle and higher secondary level and Scheduled castes (SC) and scheduled tribes (SC) during 1990 to 2007 period.

(ii) The disparity in availability of teachers during 1990 to 2007 period.

METHODOLOGY AND DATA

There are number of parameters for gender disparity in education like the age of entry into school, enrolment rate, drop-out rate, quality of education, pupil-teacher ratio, budget allocation for education, number of teachers available and number of institutions etc. to keep the study in manageable limits and availability of data from a single sources only following categories, i.e. enrolment rate of students, SC and ST community students, available teachers in general are analyzed in the present study.

The gender disparity in each level of education is calculate by the ratio of female to male (F/M ratio) enrolment (for gender disparity in enrolment), the ratio of female to male (F/M ratio) enrolment for SC/ST students, and the ratio of female to male number of teacher (for gender disparity in available teachers). The data is obtained from selected educational statistical data, 2005-06 and 2000-07 (Ministry Human Resource Development, GOI, and New Delhi).

DISCUSSION

Adult Literacy

Adult literacy rate represents estimated number of literate people aged 15 years and above expressed as a percentage of the population aged 15 years and above.

A person is considered literate if he/she can read and write with understanding a simple statement in any language. Table 1 shows that male-female gap in adult literacy of 1991- 2005 period. The male-female gap in literacy rate has decreased from 27.8 per cent in 1991 to 23 per cent 2005-06. It is indicated that more number of female persons entered in educational stream.

ENROLMENT OF ALL CATEGORIES

The gender disparity in enrolment at primary, middle and Sec, Higher secondary education level has decreased (Table 2) during 1990-91 to 2006-

Table 1
Male-Female gap in Adult literacy (15 years and above) -1991 to 2005-06

Year	*Persons*	*Male*	*Female*	*Male-Female Gap in Rate Adult Literacy*
1991 *	48.54	61.80	34.09	27.8
2001**	61.0	73.3	47.8	25.5
2005-06***	63.40	71.10	55.10	23.0

*excluding J&K.
**Census, 2001.
***National Family Health Survey-2005-06

07 period. In 1990-91, the female to male ratio (F/M ratio) of enrolment is 40.4 at primary level. It has reached to 62.5 in 2006-07. Likewise, at middle level, the gender disparity is 0.58 in 1990-91 and reached to 0.82 in 2006-07. The secondary and higher secondary school level also, the gender disparity has improved for the reference period. Even though, the entire study period, the gender disparity remained high at middle school education level when compared to primary and sec/hr secondary education.

Schedule Castes (SC) Enrolment

Educational attainments in terms of enrolment and retention generally correspond to the hierarchical order in rural India. While the upper castes have traditionally enjoyed these advantages, and they continue to so, the schedule caste and backward castes children have lagged behind in primary schooling. In this context, Table 3 illustrates gender disparity in enrolment of scheduled castes. It can be seen that, at primary level gender disparity has improved by 0.3 during the reference period. In middle school level, the gender disparity for SC's is 0.51 in 1990-91 and reached to 0.73 in 2006-07. During the study period, Sec/Higher secondary school level, the gender disparity ratios for Scheduled castes has improved marginally by the rate of 0.4.

Schedule Tribes (ST) Enrolment

Gender disparity persists among each of the population groups. The gender disparity in enrolment for ST's is given in Table 4. It is clearly show that, the gender disparity in enrolment for scheduled tribes has improved at primary, secondary and sec and higher secondary level during 1990-91 to 2006-07. But, the gender disparity for ST's has increased by only 0.3 at primary level of education when compared to other levels of education.

GENDER DISPARITY AMONG THE TEACHERS

Table 5 provides information about Female/Male ratio for teachers at different levels of education. During the study period, the gender disparity in teachers has improved by 0.3 and 0.2 at primary and middle

Table 2
Enrolment and Female / Male Ratio by Level of Education and Sex (1990-91 to 2006-07)

Year	Male (in Million)	Female (in Million)	Female-Male Ratio*	Male (in Million)	Female (in Million)	Female-Male Ratio*	Male (in Million)	Female (in Million)	Female-Male Ratio*
	Primary			Middle			Sec /Hr Secondary		
1990-91	57.0	40.4	0.70	21.5	12.5	0.58	12.8	6.3	0.49
1991-92	58.6	42.3	0.72	22.0	13.6	0.61	13.5	6.9	0.51
1992-93	57.9	41.7	0.72	21.2	12.9	0.60	13.6	6.9	0.51
1993-94	55.1	41.9	0.76	20.6	13.5	0.65	13.2	7.5	0.56
1994-95	60.0	45.1	0.75	22.1	14.3	0.64	14.2	7.9	0.56
1995- 96	60.9	46.2	0.75	22.7	14.8	0.65	14.6	8.3	0.57
1996-97	61.4	46.8	0.76	22.9	15.2	0.66	15.3	.8.7	0.57
1997-98	62.3	48.0	0.77	23.6	15.9	0.67	16.1	9.3	0.58
1998- 99	62.7	49.0	0.78	23.9	16.5	0.69	16.6	10.1	0.60
1999-00	63.6	50.0	0.79	24.3	17.0	0.69	17.2	10.8	0.62
2000-01	64.0	49.8	0.78	25.3	17.5	0.69	16.9	10.7	0.63
2001-02	63.6	50.3	0.79	28.1	18.7	0.66	18.4	12.1	0.65
2002-03	65.1	57.3	0.88	26.3	20.6	0.78	19.5	13.7	0.70
2003-04	68.4	59.9	0.93	27.3	21.5	0.79	20.6	14.4	0.70
2004-05	69.7	61.1	0.87	28.5	22.7	0.80	21.7	15.4	0.71
2005-06@	70,5	61.6	0.87	28.9	23.3	0.81	22.3	16.1	0.72
2006-07#	71.0	62.5	0.88	29.8	24.6	0.82	14.90	10.9	0.73

@ Selected Educational Statistics, 2005-06
# Provisional, Selected Educational Statistics-2006-07, MHRD, New Delhi, 2009
Ratios are calculated by authors

Table 3
Schedule Castes Enrolment and Female / Male Ratio by Level of Education and Sex (1990-91 to 2006-07)

Year	Male (000)	Female (000)	Female-Male Ratio*	Male (000)	Female (000)	Female-Male Ratio*	Male (000)	Female (000)	Female-Male Ratio*
	Primary			Middle			Sec /Hr Secondary		
1990-91	9737	6057	0.62	2747	1413	0.51	1703	635	0.37
1991-92	9709	6328	0.65	3137	1556	0.50	1878	703	0.37
1992-93	10317	7034	0.68	3478	1933	0.56	1822	709	0.39
1993-94	10412	7169	0.69	3566	2014	0.56	1981	827	0.42
1994-95	10889	7543	0.69	3330	1883	0.57	1788	803	0.45
1995- 96	11284	7892	0.70	7453	1992	0.58	1854	887	0.48
1996-97	11175	8368	0.75	3621	2176	0.60	1952	975	0.50
1997-98	12104	8759	0.72	3825	2299	0.60	2042	1050	0.51
1998- 99	12453	9185	0.73	3918	2505	0.64	2255	1221	0.54
1999-00	12296	9157	0.74	3945	2582	0.65	2389	1332	0.56
2000-01	12059	9136	0.75	4066	2628	0.65	2418	1394	0.58
2001-02	12251	9253	0.76	4551	2945	0.65	2693	1622	0.60
2002-03	11943	9726	0.81	4430	3062	0.69	2776	1624	0.59
2003-04	12764	10365	0.81	4734	3343	0.71	2938	1522	0.52
2004-05	13762	10995	0.80	5100	3597	0.71	3228	1990	0.62
2005-06@	13988	11325	0.81	5313	3834	0.72	3413	2185	0.64
2006-07#	14442	11779	0.81	5465	3988	0.73	2619	2399	0.66

@ Selected Educational Statistics, 2005-06
# Provisional, Selected Educational Statistics-2006-07, MHRD, New Delhi, 2009
Ratios are calculated by authors

Table 4

Schedule Tribes Enrolment and Female / Male Ratio by Level of Education and Sex (1990-91 to 2006-07)

Year	*Male (000)*	*Female (000)*	*Female-Male Ratio**	*Male (000)*	*Female (000)*	*Female-Male Ratio**	*Male (000)*	*Female (000)*	*Female-Male Ratio**
		Primary			*Middle*			*Sec /Hr Secondary*	
1990-91	4958	2911	0.59	1131	576	0.51	567	238	0.42
1991-92	4951	3082	0.62	1214	580	0.48	590	253	0.43
1992-93	5032	3333	0.66	1336	693	0.52	610	272	0.45
1993-94	5154	3441	0.67	1424	770	0.54	682	315	0.46
1994-95	5454	3605	0.66	1377	871	0.63	779	350	0.45
1995- 96	5589	3826	0.68	1448	837	0.58	765	359	0.47
1996-97	5896	4057	0.69	1508	894	0.59	790	385	0.49
1997-98	6141	4311	0.70	1643	996	0.61	823	417	0.51
1998- 99	6225	4452	0.71	1698	1026	0.60	909	464	0.51
1999-00	6532	4728	0.72	1802	1106	0.61	980	500	0.51
2000-01	6330	4665	0.74	1879	1205	0.64	955	535	0.56
2001-02	6691	5040	0.75	2054	1306	0.64	1079	622	0.58
2002-03	6422	5408	0.84	1913	1320	0.68	1105	678	0.61
2003-04	6776	5741	0.85	2136	1526	0.71	1222	729	0.60
2004-05	7367	6369	0.86	2395	1776	0.74	1290	795	0.62
2005-06@	7513	6601	0.88	2516	1950	0.78	1340	863	0.64
2006-07#	7628	6783	0.89	2605	2059	0.79	1668	951	0.62

@ Selected Educational Statistics, 2005-06

Provisional, Selected Educational Statistics-2006-07, MHRD, New Delhi, 2009

Ratios are calculated by authors

Table 5
Teachers and Female / Male Ratio by Level of Education and Sex (1990-91 to 2006-07)

Year	*Male (000)*	*Female (000)*	*Female-Male Ratio**	*Male (000)*	*Female (000)*	*Female-Male Ratio**	*Male (000)*	*Female (000)*	*Female-Male Ratio**
	Primary			*Middle*			*Sec /Hr Secondary*		
1990-91	1143	473	0.41	717	356	0.50	917	417	0.45
1991-92	1152	492	0.42	714	365	0.51	931	450	0.48
1992-93	1137	514	0.45	709	376	0.53	941	454	0.48
1993-94	1110	513	0.46	723	406	0.56	953	492	0.52
1994-95	1157	531	0.46	746	410	0.55	986	495	0.50
1995- 96	1176	558	0.47	758	624	0.56	1030	519	0.50
1996-97	1190	566	0.48	769	431	0.56	1069	544	0.51
1997-98	1226	597	0.49	793	444	0.56	1086	558	0.51
1998- 99	1233	605	0.49	821	478	0.57	1129	581	0.51
1999-00	1245	643	0.52	852	475	0.56	1185	598	0.50
2000-01	1221	675	0.55	820	506	0.62	1184	577	0.49
2001-02	1213	715	0.59	921	547	0.59	1157	620	0.53
2002-03	1167	746	0.64	936	645	0.69	1221	812	0.66
2003-04	1260	837	0.66	944	648	0.69	1250	774	0.62
2004-05	1390	842	0.64	992	597	0.60	1282	801	0.62
2005-06@	1326	858	0.65	998	673	0.67	1333	821	0.62
2006-07#	1339	892	0.67	993	664	0.69	1668	951	0.57

@ Selected Educational Statistics, 2005-06
# Provisional, Selected Educational Statistics-2006-07, MHRD, New Delhi, 2009
Ratios are calculated by authors

level of education respectively. The female to male ratio at secondary and higher secondary level has decreased from 0.64 in 2005-06 to 0.62 in 2006-07.

CONCLUSION

In general, at all the level of education, the gender disparity in enrolment for all categories of students, SC's and ST's students have not improved gradually (i.e., some years F/M ratios has increased or decreased). Over all, the gender disparity is higher among the SC's and ST's when compare to all categories of enrolment. The gender disparity in teachers is higher at sec and higher secondary level of education as compared to other levels of education such as primary and middle level. Hence, the study suggested that, the government policy to stress on girls education at primary level should be expanded by including middle and secondary and higher secondary level. The quality of education in the form of qualified female teachers, good physical infrastructure of schools and low cost schooling, reasonable student- teacher ratio etc is needed.

"To educate girls is reduce poverty, study after study has taught us that there is no tool for development more effective than the education of girls".

Kofi Annan, U.N. Secretay General

REFERENCES

"Analysis of Disparity to Access EFA Progress Hand-on Training Session-EFA mid-Decade Assessment Report-06-07", Feb-2006, Tangok, Myanmar.

Annual Status of Education Report, (2006), New Delhi. *www.indiatogether.org*.

Belkachia, Said, "Monitoring Gender Equality in Framework of Education for All", Working Paper No. 11, Statistical Commission for Europe, Geneva, 23-25, Sept 2002.

George Ingram et al., "The Untapped Opportunity, How Public-Private Partnerships can Advance Education for All", AED-*www.aed.org*, accessed on 20.10.08.

Lukas, Jr, R.E. (1993), Making a Miracle, Econometric a, 61(2), (March).

Lewis, Maureen and Lockheed, (2007), "Marlaine, Inexcusable Absence: Why 60 Million Girls Still aren't in School and What to do about it," Centre for Global Development, Washington D.C.

Schultz, T. Paul (1993), "Return to Women's Education, in E.M. King and M.A. Hill (eds), Women's Education in Developing Countries: Barriers, Benefits and Policies", John Hopkin University Press, Baltimore.

Social and Rural Research Institution of IMRB International, (2005), "A Report on Out-of-School Children", Report Commissioned by the Ministry of Human Resource Development of India, New Delhi.

Thomas (1990), "Intra Household Resource Allocation: An International Approach", *Journal of Human Resources*, 25(4).

UNICEF, (1999), "State of World's Children 1999, Oxford University Press, Oxford.

Vandemoortale, J. and Delamonica E., (2000), "'Education 'Vaccine' against HIV/AIDS", Current Issues in Comparative Education.

World Bank, (2004), "Project Appraisal Document: Elementary Education Project", Report 27703-in, World Bank, Washington D.C.

www.Unescobkk.org/aims/Education/Stats, accessed on 14.7.09.

Zaidi, S.M.I.A, "An Measures of Inequality", *www.Education for all India.com*, accessed on 14.7.09.

9

CASTE AND LABOUR MARKET DISCRIMINATION IN TAMIL NADU

V. SIVASANKAR

INTRODUCTION

The Scheduled Castes (SCs) and Scheduled Tribes (STs) were constituted 16 per cent and 8 per cent respectively in 2001 Census. The constitution of India provided a special protection to interest of these groups even though they discriminated in accessing jobs in government and private. Often they get less skilled and low paid jobs compared to the other social groups and as a result they are economically backward. This paper examines the labour market discrimination of STs, SCs, OBCs and Others in Tamil Nadu. The reason for the selection of Tamil Nadu has that the state which had strong social movements like Dravidian movement which was started early 1940s. Further, Tamil Nadu has pioneering to implement in OBCs reservation in educational institutions and government jobs. This paper examines the inequalities in labour market among different social groups.

Data for this study have been taken from the 50th (1993-94), 55th (1999-00) and 61st (2004-05) rounds of National Sample Survey Organisation (NSSO). This paper is divided into five sections: Section I estimates population distribution according to caste groups. Section II explores the inequality in access to education. Section III describes the labour force participation among social groups. Section IV looks at the status of employment among social groups. Section V explores the work force participation (employment) among social groups. Section VI describes the pattern of unemployment among social groups.

SECTION I

POPULATION DISTRIBUTION ACCORDING TO CASTE GROUPS

According to Census, 56 per cent of Tamil Nadu's Population was rural and remaining 44 per cent was urban. Among social groups, SCs were 23.79 per cent and STs were 1.58 per cent in rural and in urban it was 12.91

per cent and 0.36 per cent respectively. The NSSO is also collected an information on population and it classified into different social groups such as STs, SCs, OBCs and Others. The others consists of all upper caste Hindus and other religious groups. The NSS, 61st round in 2004-05 shows that the OBCs were highest proportions and STs were lowest proportion both in rural and urban (see Table 1). The proportion of OBCs were 70.54 per cent, SCs were 27.06 per cent Others were 1.86 per cent and STs were 0.54 per cent in rural areas. Similarly, in urban areas were 74.74 per cent, 14.52 per cent, 10.09 per cent and 0.64 per cent respectively. The obvious fact is that the proportions of STs are lowest representation in rural and urban areas. But the NSSO report over estimated in urban STs and lower estimated in rural compared to Census report even though the Census was 2001 and NSSO 61st round 2004-05. Further, National Family Health Survey (NFHs) also classified population into religion and caste wise. The religion wise are Hindus, Muslims, Christians, Sikh, Buddhist, Jain and others and caste wise are STs, SCs, OBCs and Others. According to NFHs-

Table 1
Population Distribution according to Social Groups 2004-05

Social Groups	*Rural*	*Urban*
STs	0.54	0.64
SCs	27.06	14.52
OBCs	70.54	74.74
Others	1.86	10.09

Source: Report on Household Consumer Expenditure among Socio-Economic Groups, 2004-05, 61st Report No.514

3, STs proportions were 0.8 per cent, SCs were 22.2 per cent, OBCs were 74.5 per cent and Other were only 2.4 per cent.

SECTION II

INEQUALITY OF LITERACY AND EDUCATIONAL STATUS AMONG SOCIAL GROUPS

The 55th NSSO (1999-00) Report No.473 provided literacy and level of education in India. The information covered the level of education among different classes, religion and social groups. This report consists literate and not literate and the literate again disaggregated into below primary, primary, middle, secondary, higher secondary and graduate and above. Table 2 show the level of illiterate and literate among different social groups. The urban Tamil Nadu has more literate in all social groups than rural Tamil Nadu and it means that the number of illiterate is more in rural Tamil Nadu. Among gender, more illiterate are female both in rural and urban areas than the male and also rural female are significantly illiterate in all social groups. The gender gap is wider among SCs and STs and not as much gap among OBCs and Others social groups. Among rural literate population, the Others have more literate and followed by OBCs both male and female. Among SCs and STs, STs have substantially lower level of literate than SCs both male and female. In contrary, urban STs have significantly higher literate than Others, OBCs and SCs. Further urban SCs have low level of literate than any social groups.

Table 2
Percentage of Illiterate and Literate among Social Groups in Tamil Nadu

Social Groups	*STs*		*SCs*		*OBCs*		*Others*	
Gender	*Male*	*Female*	*Male*	*Female*	*Male*	*Female*	*Male*	*Female*
			Rural Tamil Nadu					
Illiterate	39.2	60.1	33.1	55.1	23.2	44.2	10.1	26.2
Literate	60.8	39.9	66.9	44.9	76.8	55.8	89.9	73.8
			Urban Tamil Nadu					
Illiterate	2.9	6.0	18.6	32.8	9.5	22.7	3.9	10.3
Literate	97.1	94.0	81.4	67.2	90.5	77.3	96.1	89.7

Source: Report on Literacy and Level of Education in India 1999-00, NSS Report No.473

The level of education of different social groups is given is given Table 3. It can be noted that the percentage graduates and above more in urban areas than rural areas. In gender perspective male graduates are more than female graduates both in rural and urban areas. By examining the tendency of education level among different social groups, it is possible to obtain some fact. The fact is that the proportion of graduates and above more in male STs than others social groups both in rural and urban areas. Similarly, urban female STs are more graduates than others social groups.

SECTION III

LABOUR FORCE PARTICIPATION AMONG SOCIAL GROUPS

Labour force or the 'economically active' persons refers to the population which supplies or seeks to supply labour for production and therefore, includes both the 'employed' and the 'unemployed'. The labour force participation rate (LFPR), presented in (usual status) Table 4 for Tamil Nadu. The proportion of economically active person was the higher among STs, followed by the SCs, OBCs and Others both in rural and urban areas. The male-female differences in LFPR were prominent in all the categories of households. Between rural and urban, the labour force participation rate was high in rural areas both male and female in all social groups. Among females the LFPR was the lowest among Others Social groups in rural and urban areas.

Table 3
Educational Profile of Social Groups

Social Groups	*Below Primary*	*Primary*	*Middle*	*Secondary*	*Higher Secondary*	*Graduates & Above*
			Rural Male			
STs	16.9	23.6	6.2	7.5	2.8	3.8
SCs	22.3	19.1	14.4	7.2	2.5	1.3
OBCs	21.4	21.6	16.5	10.6	4.0	2.7
Others	19.1	27.1	17.1	15.5	7.5	3.6
All	21.5	21.1	15.9	9.8	3.7	2.3
			Rural Female			
STs	11.0	10.9	7.7	6.1	3.7	0.4
SCs	15.5	14.2	9.8	3.8	1.3	0.3
OBCs	17.5	16.8	11.3	5.9	3.1	1.3
Others	21.3	23.9	11.3	10.2	6.1	1.1
All	17.0	16.3	10.9	5.5	2.7	1.0
			Urban Male			
STs	8.3	11.7	17.2	17.4	10.1	32.4
SCs	16.8	22.9	20.4	11.7	5.9	3.8
OBCs	14.9	20.3	20.2	18.1	8.7	8.4
Others	9.9	13.0	14.5	22.8	11.5	24.4
All	14.1	19.2	19.1	18.1	9.0	11.0
			Urban Female			
STs	21.9	12.9	18.7	16.9	8.3	15.4
SCs	16.6	19.3	18.6	17.6	3.9	1.3
OBCs	15.9	19.8	16.0	12.9	7.7	5.1
Others	15.1	14.7	14.7	16.7	9.9	18.7
All	15.9	16.1	16.1	13.0	7.6	7.2

Source: Report on Literacy and Level of Education in India 1999-00, NSS Report No.473

Table 4
Labour Force Participation Rate (LFPR) for Different Social Groups

Social Groups	*STs*		*SCs*		*OBCs*		*Others*	
Gender	*Male*	*Female*	*Male*	*Female*	*Male*	*Female*	*Male*	*Female*
				Rural Tamil Nadu				
1993	55.6	47.0	62.6	55.0			61.0	45.6
1999-00	66.6	56.8	53.2	28.7	62.1	41.6	58.4	21.9
2004-05	61.5	59.8	58.0	48.0	61.3	46.4	58.9	25.9
				Urban Tamil Nadu				
1993	68.4	19.8	57.2	31.6			60.4	23.6
1999-00	50.5	27.2	55.7	28.5	60.3	22.9	54.0	17.2
2004-05	57.3	33.9	58.8	33.7	61.7	25.0	60.1	15.0

Source: NSSO Report No.425, 469 and 516.

SECTION IV

STATUS OF EMPLOYMENT AMONG SOCIAL GROUPS

The status of rural workforce was divided in to two: self-employment and wage employment. That self-employment further divided into self-employment in agriculture and self-employed in non-agriculture. Similarly wage employment is divided into agricultural labour and other labour and other labour. The urban stat of workforce is also distinction between self-employment and wage employment. The wage employment is divided into wage/salaried employment and causal employment. The status distribution of the workforce in Tamil Nadu is presented in Table 5.

Table 5
Status of Employment

Status	*1993*			*1999-00*				*2004-05*			
	STs	*SCs*	*Others*	*STs*	*SCs*	*OBCs*	*Others*	*STs*	*SCs*	*OBCs*	*Others*
				Rural Tamil Nadu							
Self-Employed in Agriculture	26.1	6.5	25.3	26.1	5.8	21.6	18.7	10.0	10.1	24.4	19.8
Self-Employed in Non-Agriculture	4.7	4.3	16.2	7.0	6.0	15.3	14.0	8.7	7.6	15.6	22.3
Agricultural Labour	50.8	70.6	31.8	43.6	67.0	36.1	21.2	66.0	55.9	28.4	8.1
				Urban Tamil Nadu							
Self-Employed	16.4	15.2	30.3	11.8	14.6	31.6	30.6	31.7	18.8	35.5	31.8
Regular/ Salaried	26.6		41.2	34.1	29.6	42.6	53.3	29.2	44.4	43.2	45.2
Causal Labour	43.4	16.2	15.9	42.6	36.4	17.9	4.1	35.6	25.5	12.7	1.4

Source: NSSO Report NO.425, 469 and 516

STATUS OF RURAL WORK FORCE

The proportion of self-employed in agriculture among groups was maximum of OBCs and minimum of SCs households (see Table 5). The proportion of self-employed in agriculture among OBCs were increased from 21.6 per cent in 1999-00 to 24.4 per cent, others were 18.7 per cent to 19.8 per cent and SCs were 5.8 per cent to 10.1 per cent respectively. However, the proportion of self-employed in agriculture among STs were sharply declined to 26.1 per cent in 1993 to 10.0 per cent among STs were sharply declined to 26.1 per cent in 1993-00 to 10.0 per cent in 2004-05.

The proportion of self-employed in non-agriculture among social group's in rural areas recorded dissimilar increase. For STs were 4.7 per cent in 1993 to 7.0 per cent to 1999-00 and to 8.7 per cent in 2004-05. The correspondingly, SCs were 4.3 per cent, 6.0 per cent, and 7.6 per cent. The OBCs position was stable between 1999-00 and 2004-05, which was 15.6 per cent. But the proportion of self-employed in non agriculture among Others were soaring from 14.0 per cent in 199-00 to 22.3 per cent in 2004-05.

The tendency for agriculture labour among all social groups was declined expects STs. But the declining proportion among OBCs and others were a great extent and SCs were tiny. The proportion of agricultural labour among STs were declined from 50.8 per cent to 43.6 per cent in 1993 to 1999-00 and then swelled to 66.0 per cent in 2004.05. The proportions of agricultural labour households of SCs were fall from 70.6 per cent in 1993 to 67.0 per cent in 199-00 and again decline 55.9 per cent. Meanwhile, OBCs and Others were sharp fall of agricultural labour: OBCs were 36.1 per cent in 199-00 to 28.4 per cent and Others category were 21.2 per cent to 8.1 per cent respective.

This gives that the proportion of agricultural labour among STs were increased SCs were declined. In order to understand the cause, we examine the landholding patterns among social groups. The proportion of landless households among social groups in rural Tamil Nadu is shown in the Table 6. The proportions of landless households among STs were increased and SCs were declined. The growing landless households among STs were bound to agricultural labour. Correspondingly, the proportion of landless labour also increased in Others category also. But they bound to self-employed in non-agricultural work. The obvious features of the increased landholdings among SCs households. However predominant SCs households were marginal landholdings (see Table 7) 73.6 per cent of landholding households were marginal groups. Among marginal landholdings, SCs were 83.9 per cent, OBCs were 70.7 per cent, STs were 65.5 per cent and Other social groups were 50.3 per cent.

Table 6
Percentage of Landless Households among Social Groups

Years	*STs*	*SCs*	*Others*
1987-88	15.9	24.7	16.2
1993-94	18.4	24.8	19.5
1999-00	11.1	15.1	10.2
2003	24.0	13.8	26.6

Source: Various NSSO Rounds

Table 7
Distribution of Land among Social Groups 2003

Size Class	*STs*	*SCs*	*OBCs*	*Others*	*All*
Landless	24.0	13.8	17.2	26.6	16.5
Marginal	65.5	83.9	70.7	50.3	73.6
Small	7.8	1.8	7.0	8.6	5.7
Semi-Medium	2.7	0.5	3.5	12.2	2.9
Medium	0.0	0.0	1.6	2.1	1.2
Large	0.0	0.0	0.1	0.0	0.0
All	100.0	100	100	100	100

Source: Report on Household Ownership Holdings in India, 2003, 59th round, NSS Report No.491.

STATUS OF URBAN WORK FORCE

The urban workforce status of household of different social groups is above in Table 5. The table shows that the higher incidence of causal labour was among the STs followed by the SCs. The share of causal labour among Others category was very small and followed by OBCs. Although the proportion of causal labour among STs were slightly decline from 43.4 per cent in 1993 to 42.6 per cent in 1999-00 and then shows sharp fall to 35.6 per cent in 2004-05. For SCs the proportion of causal labour was sharply rose 16.2 per cent to 36.4 per cent during the 1993 -94 to 1999-00 and at decline to 25.5 per cent in 2004-05. The proportion of OBCs was 17.9 per cent in 1999-00 and to fall 12.7 per cent in 2004-05. Similarly the Others were 4.1 per cent and 1.4 per cent in above respective periods.

The proportions of self-employed among OBCs were uppermost followed by Others social category and the SCs was bottom. For OBCs 31.6 per cent in 1999-00 and to 35.5 per cent in 2004-05 and the similar trend for Others also which was 30.6 per cent to 31.8 per cent respectively. The proportions of self-employed among STs were fall during the late 1990s (1999-00). This was 16.4 per cent in 1993 to 11.8 per cent in 1999-00 and to mount in 2004-05, which was 31.7 per cent. For SCs, the proportions of self-employed were declined 15.2 per cent to 14.6 per cent during 1993 to 1999-00 and latter increased to 18.8 per cent in 2004-05.

The grater proportions of regular and salaried worker were Others category and followed by SCs. This can be noted that the proportion of regular and salaried households among SCs were increased from 29.6 per cent to 44.4 per cent in 1999-00 to 2004-05 and the same time OBCs were increased a slightly from 42.6 per cent to 43.2 per cent during the period. In a contrary, the Other social groups were highest proportion of regular and salaried worker but their proportion were declined 53.3 per cent in 1999-00 to 45.2 per cent 2004-05. Among STs proportions had increased in 1999-00 and to fall in 2004-05, which was 34.1 per cent and 29.2 per cent respectively.

SECTION V

WORKFORCE PARTICIPATION (LEVEL OF EMPLOYMENT)

The proportion of person employed according to usual status (ps+ss) in rural and urban Tamil Nadu is shown in the Table 8. Both in rural and urban Tami Nadu the worker-population ratio (WPR) had increased from 1993 to 2004-05. For male and female, the male worker population ratio is highest. Among social groups, STs were higher than SCs, OBCs and Others social groups. Between rural and urban, the urban WPR was lower than rural and the fact was that the working age population in urban areas to attend schools and colleges compared to the rural areas. The sharp increased WPR during 1999-00 to 2004-05 was distressed in income aspects. The downward trend of agricultural wage rate and sluggish trend of urban wage rate would lead to search of employment both male and female, particularly the old aged persons (60 and above) enter into labour market. And as a result the work-population rate increased in Tamil Nadu.

Table 8
Worker-Population Ratio in Rural Tamil Nadu and Rural India

Social Groups	*STs*		*SCs*		*OBCs*		*Others*	
Gender	*Male*	*Female*	*Male*	*Female*	*Male*	*Female*	*Male*	*Female*
			Rural Tamil Nadu					
1993	40.8	43.4	47.8	49.3			35.2	35.2
1999-00	65.6	55.0	56.3	45.8	60.9	41.2	57.0	20.8
2004-05	61.5	59.8	57.0	47.0	60.7	45.9	58.9	25.0
			Urban Tamil Nadu					
1993	1.01		10.9	12.5			3.8	3.8
1999-00	47.7	27.2	52.5	27.9	58.3	21.6	523	16.1
2004-05	57.3	33.9	56.5	32.0	59.8	23.8	59.5	14.7

Source: NSSO Reporı No. 425, 469 and 516

SECTION VI

UNEMPLOYMENT AMONG SOCIAL GROUPS

Table 9 show that the level of unemployment (ps+ss) in rural and urban areas of Tamil Nadu. Urban unemployment is more than rural unemployment in all social groups. This below measurements shows that the level of open unemployment (UPS). The proportions of unemployment have been decline from 1993 to 2004-05 in all social groups in rural and urban areas. Among social groups, highest rate of unemployment exit among SCs and it lowest among STs in rural and urban. But in underemployment (current daily status) had increased sharply among all social groups in Tamil Nadu.

Table 9
Level of Unemployment (UPS)

Social Groups	*STs*		*SCs*		*OBCs*		*Others*	
Gender	*Male*	*Female*	*Male*	*Female*	*Male*	*Female*	*Male*	*Female*
			Rural Tamil Nadu					
1993-94	0.4	0.1	2.6	0.6			1.4	0.5
1999-00	2.0	1.8	2.3	0.1	1.4	0.5	1.4	1.6
2004-05	0.0	0.0	1.0	0.4	0.6	0.6	0.0	0.9
			Urban Tamil Nadu					
1993-94	3.8	0.0	3.3	1.8			2.9	1.9
1999-00	2.8	0.0	3.6	0.8	2.1	1.3	1.9	1.1
2004-05	0.0	0.0	2.3	1.7	1.9	1.2	0.6	0.3

Source: NSSO Report NO.425, 469 and 516

CONCLUSION

Our result suggest that wide variation in labour markets discrimination across Tamil Nadu may be because of factors: changing landholding patterns and increasing landless labour in rural areas, increasing causalisation of urban labour markets. Another important feature is that level of education among different social groups. There is empirical evidence of significant gap among STs, SCs, OBCs and Others in participation of work force and status of employment. Among SCs and STs, urban STs are better than urban SCs and rural SCs are better than rural STs. Tamil Nadu SCs and STs are better than all India level of SCs and STs. The SCs and STs have engaged in low status work such as agricultural labour in rural areas and causal in urban areas compared to OBCs and Other social groups. However, the gaps have been gradually declined in recent years.

REFERENCES

Banerjee, B. and J.B. Knight (1985), 'Caste and Discrimination in the Indian Labour Market', *Journal of Development Economics*, Vol. 17.

Madheswaran and Attewell Pauul (2007), 'Caste Discrimination in the Indian Urban Labour Market: Evidence from the National Sample Survey', *Economic and Political Weekly*, Vol. 41, No. 42.

Mohanty, M. (2006), 'Social Inequality, Labour Market Dynamics and the Need for Expanding Reservation: Some Issues for Consideration', Working Paper No. 594, Indian Institute of Management, Calcutta.

National Sample Survey Organisation: Round No 43rd, 50th, 55th and 61st Employment and Unemployment Report.

National Sample Survey Organisation (2003), Report No. 491, Household Ownership Holdings in India.

National Sample Survey Organisation (1999-00), Report No. 473, Literacy and Level of Education in India.

Thorat, S.K. (2001), 'Caste and Economic Discrimination: Theory and Evidence on Rural Labour Market', *Arthavijnana*, Vol. 4, No. 1-2.

Thorat, S.K. (2005), '*Reservation Policy for Private Sector: Why and How* ', Sugava Prakashan, Pune.

10

DISPARITIES AMONG SOCIAL GROUPS IN EMPLOYMENT AND WAGE RATES IN INDIA

R. M. Jagannathan

INTRODUCTION

There are differences in the wage and earning in the labour market which directly leads to impoverishment in many dimensions and not in a straight forward fashion. The poor are likely to be excluded from wider participation in society, due to their relative material disadvantage in terms of income. However, discrimination many also lead to deprivation as the poor people may be excluded from both means of livelihood as their lands are commercialized, traditional occupations become redundant with technological advances and also from capability formation which prevents their movement into the mainstream of development.

The Scheduled Caste and the Scheduled Tribe are the out-castes in the development process of India for quite a long time. In recent times, the issue of the development of the SC & STs has once again come to centre stage in view of the debate on reservation. And also, the process of globalization is most likely to affect the labour market as it is leading to greater social inequality in wage earnings. This link between liberalization and earning disparity is analysed in this paper.

SOCIAL DISPARITY IN WAGE AND EARNINGS - A REVIEW

It is argued that earning differentials is nothing but inequality generated by the workings of the economic system and is termed social only to conceal its economic origin. On the other hand, disparity appears s people are evicted from spaces they previously occupied or are deprived of rights of access in the first place due to international processes and institutional relationships associated with rapid social and economic global change and local impacts and responses. Most of the empirical studies conclude that at least there has been an erosion of social equity in recent times and State intervention is necessary for bringing the disadvantaged groups nearer to the advantaged ones, especially in the developing countries.

Studies made at the regional level use the methodological approaches based on rights, groups and institutions.

In India, disparities across social classes have been studied by few researchers in recent times. However, most of them have either analysed discrimination from the gender angle or have explored existing levels of poverty among social groups and how poverty among certain groups have been consistently higher than the rest. Only a few studies have looked into the social disparities in the labour market in India. Banerjee and Knight examined wage differentials between scheduled and non-scheduled castes in the urban labour market and Borooah et al examined differences in employment rates between upper and backward castes. Takahiro also studies the caste discrimination in the labour market in north India, which indicates that job discrimination against the backward classes does happen.

In this background, this paper attempts to analyse the trends in wages and earning differentials among social groups in Indian labour market and also explore the social disparities at the regional level in India.

The necessary data for this paper have been collected from the surveys of NSSO pertaining to 50th, 55th and 62nd (the latest round available) rounds made in the years 1993-94, 1999-2000 and 2005-06.

DIFFERENCES IN EMPLOYMENT AND WAGES AMONG SOCIAL GROUPS IN INDIA

The differences that exist among the social groups in India in the employment is explained with the help of the data presented in Table 1.

Table 1
Shares in Employment among Social Groups in India

Social Groups	*Share in Population*			*Share in Employment*		
	1993-94	*1999-2000*	*2005-06*	*1993-94*	*1999-2000*	*2005-06*
Scheduled Caste	18.4	19.6	19.7	26.0	20.6	25.6
Scheduled Tribe	8.4	8.9	8.5	10.5	8.5	9.7
Non-SC&ST	73.2	71.4	71.8	63.5	70.9	64.7
Total	100.0	100.0	100.0	100.0	100.0	100.0

Source: NSSO Reports on Employment and Unemployment, 1997, 2001 and 2007.

The shares of social groups in total population and employment during the post-reform period indicates that the share of the SC group in the total population has gone up continuously from 18.4 per cent to 19.6 per cent and further to 19.7 per cent in 1993-94, 1999-2000 and 2005-06 respectively. Similarly, the share of ST population in the total has increased from 8.4 per cent to 8.9 per cent, though has declined to 8.5 per cent in 2005-06. Thus, the share of Non-SC&ST, which declined initially from 73.2 per cent to 71.4 per cent between 1993-94 and 1999-2000, has increased marginally to 71.8 per cent in 2005-06. However, the table indicates that in the post-reform period, the share in employment of the SC and ST groups has decreased drastically, especially between 1993-94 and 1999-2000. In the case of SC group, the share in employment has declined from 26 per cent to 20.6 per cent, though it has gone up again and touched 25.6 per cent in 2005-06. A similar trend could be witnessed among the ST group, as their share in employment has declined from 10.5 per cent to 8.5 per cent, but has gone up to 9.7 per cent. Thus, the share of Non-SC&ST in employment shows the reverse trend, as it increased initially from 63.5 per cent to 70.9 per cent, before declining to 64.7 per cent in 2005-06. This clearly suggests a mixed trend as far as the shares in employment during the post-reform period is concerned. These changing shares in employment among the social groups are graphically shown in Chart 1.

Chart 1: Percentage Share in Employment among Social Groups

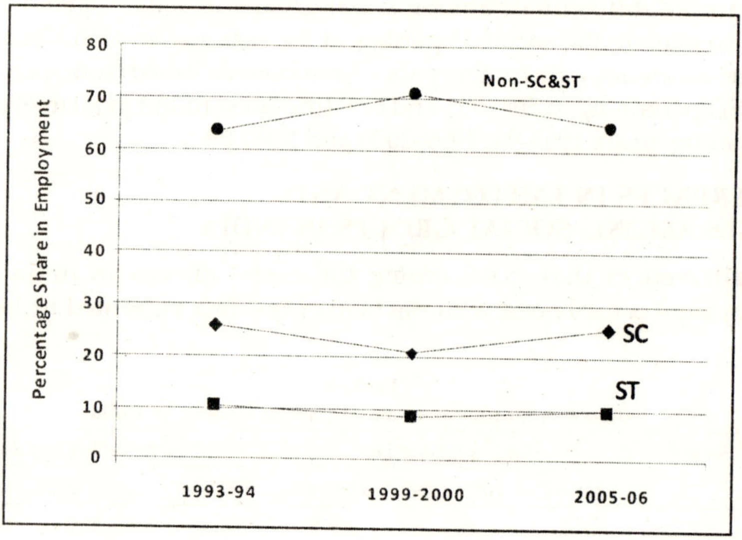

Source: Based on Table 1.

There have been commensurate changes in the shares of wages among the social groups as well. It is always better to achieve equitable employment opportunities among various sections of the population, though available evidence suggests to the contrary. Apart from equitable employment opportunities, equitable wage levels among the different social groups, is another important aspect of the labour market, which can ensure equitable living conditions among the same. However, the arrival of economic reforms and the onset of globalisation have affected the labour market in various ways. The wage levels of the employed have gone up tremendously, particularly after the arrival of the multi-national companies, along with the fact that the required qualification too has gone up considerably even at the entry level. This has led to the creation of a huge informalised and marginalised labour market, where relatively low quality jobs are paid very low wages, with clear hire and fire policy. Table 2 provides the wage shares among the social groups in India.

Table 2
Shares in Wage Earnings among Social Groups in India

Social Groups	*Share in Employment*		
	1993-94	*1999-2000*	*2005-06*
Scheduled Caste	18.0	14.3	17.5
Scheduled Tribe	6.8	5.6	5.8
Non-SC&ST	75.1	80.1	76.7
Total	100.0	100.0	100.0

Source: NSSO Reports on Employment and Unemployment, 1997, 2001 and 2007.

The wage shares among the social groups in India between the period 1993-94 and 2005-06 indicates that there have been fluctuations similar to that of the shares in employment. The wage share of SC group has declined from 18 per cent in 1993-94 to 14.3 per cent in 1999-2000, but has gone up to 17.5 per cent in 2005-06. In the case of ST group, their wage share has declined initially from 6.8 per cent to 5.6 per cent, but has gone up marginally to 5.8 per cent during the same period. Thus, the wage share of Non-SC&ST increased from 75.1 per cent in 1993-94 to 80.1 per cent in 1999-2000, but has come down to 76.7 per cent in 2005-06. This implies that the marginalised group which includes the SC and ST workforce, even when they get jobs, they earn relatively less than the Non-SC&ST group. The disparity is also alarmingly high when the groups are classified on the basis of per worker wage rate and per man-day wage rate, which is shown in Table 3.

Table 3
Wage Rate Differentials among Social Groups in India

(Figures in Rupees)

Social Groups	*Per Worker Wage Rate*			*Per Man-day Wage Rate*		
	1993-94	*1999-2000*	*2005-06*	*1993-94*	*1999-2000*	*2005-06*
Scheduled Caste	251	324	341	36	57	61
Scheduled Tribe	236	309	308	34	53	55
Non-SC&ST	432	600	838	62	102	132
Total	365	467	497	52	80	83

Source: NSSO Reports on Employment and Unemployment, 1997, 2001 and 2007.

The wage differentials among social groups given in terms of wage rate per worker and wage rate per man-day for the periods 1993-94, 1999-2000 and 2005-06 indicate huge disparities among them. The wage rate per worker (per week) in 1993-94 for the SC group was Rs. 251 that of ST was Rs. 236, while that of Non-SC&ST group was Rs. 432 and this disparities only aggravated during 1999-2000, since the ratio of the wage rate of SC and ST and Non-SC&ST has increased. The per worker wage rate per week for the SC group stood at Rs. 324 that of ST at Rs. 309, while the per worker wage rate per week of Non-SC&ST workers stood at Rs. 600. In 2005-06, the mean wage rate among the social groups further widened as shown in the table. The wage rate per man-day among the social groups is also given in the above table for the three periods. It implies that the per man-day wage rate of the SC worker stood at Rs. 36, Rs. 34 among the ST workers and Rs. 62 in the case of Non-SC&ST workers. This suggests tremendous disparities in the mean wage rate per man-day at the all-India level. In 1999-2000, the gap between the groups further accentuated, as the mean wage rate of SC worker was Rs. 57, Rs. 53 in the case of ST worker and Rs. 102 among the Non-SC&ST workers. Thus, the mean wage rates of all three groups have increased between these periods, though the rate of increase differs a lot among them. The rate of increase in the wage rate of SC and ST worker was less than the rate of increase in the wage rate of Non-SC&ST workers. This is even truer in 2005-06, as shown in the table. The per man-day wage rate of SC worker has gone up to Rs. 59, that of ST worker has moved up to Rs. 53 and the per man-day wage rate of Non-SC&ST workers has increased to Rs. 132. This underscores the fact that though per man-day wage rates of the social groups have increased, they have not moved up in a similar rate, which has aggravated the gap between them. This is graphically portrayed in Chart 2.

Chart 2: Wage Differentials among Social Groups in India

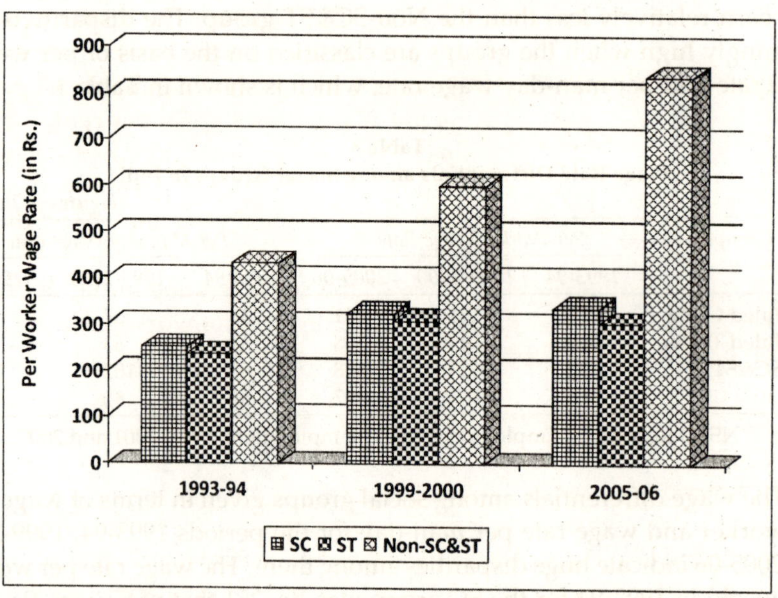

Source: Based on Table 3.

The differing rates of rise in the wage rates among the social groups at the all-India level during the post-reform period as portrayed in Chart – 2, undeniably shows that the gap in the wage rates between the SC, ST and Non-SC&ST workers has gone up over the years. Thus, it can be stated that the workers belonging to the SC and ST groups are engaged in low-quality and thus, low-paid employment, while workers belonging to Non-SC&ST group are employed in high-quality and high-paid jobs. This can be further understood by analysing the shares of social groups in both bottom of the wage and top of the wage class over the period, which is given in Table 4.

Table 4
Share of Workforce among Social Groups in India

Social Groups	*In Top Wage Class*			*In Bottom Wage Class*		
	1993-94	*1999-2000*	*2005-06*	*1993-94*	*1999-2000*	*2005-06*
Scheduled Caste	251	324	341	36	57	61
Scheduled Caste	3.5	6.6	9.7	29.8	23.8	30.4
Scheduled Tribe	1.9	3.9	3.7	12.9	11.2	13.7
Non-SC&ST	94.6	89.5	86.6	57.3	65.0	55.9
Total	100.0	100.0	100.0	100.0	100.0	100.0

Source: NSSO Reports on Employment and Unemployment, 1997, 2001 and 2007.

The data provided in Table 4 indicates that the share of workforce of the social groups in both top wage class and bottom wage class differ alarmingly over the years. In 1993-94, the share of workforce among the SC workers in the top wage class comprised of only 3.5 per cent, 1.9 per cent among the ST workers, while it was as high as 94.6 per cent among the Non-SC&ST workers. However, this gap among the social groups has come down in 1999-2000, as the shares stood at 6.6 per cent, 3.9 per cent and 89.5 per cent respectively and further down to 9.7 per cent, 3.7 per cent and 86.6 per cent in 2005-06. Thus, the gap among the workers belonging to the social groups has declined over the years, though the remaining disparities are quite significant.

The share of the workforce of the social groups in the bottom of the wage class is much more revealing. The share of workers belonging to the SC workforce was 29.8 per cent, 12.9 per cent in the case of ST workers and only 57.3 per cent in the case of Non-SC&ST workers. This gap among the social groups further increased, as the share of the workers belonging to the SC and ST workers in the bottom wage class has gone up vis-*a-vis* Non-SC&ST workers, particularly in 2005-06. This again brings home the fact that the workers belonging to the SC and ST groups are engaged in low-quality jobs as mentioned earlier, while the Non-SC&ST workers have garnered the high-quality and thus high-paid jobs in the post-globalisation situation at the all-India level.

DISPARITIES AMONG SOCIAL GROUPS AT THE REGIONAL LEVEL

Disparities among the social groups exist not only at the national level, but also at the state level, though such disparities obviously differ among the states. Table 5 presents the disparities in the earning ratio among the social groups among the major states of India in 1999-2000 and 2005-06.

Table 5
Disparities among Social Groups in Earning Ratio in Major States

States	*1999-2000*			*2005-06*		
	SC	*ST*	*Non SC&ST*	*SC*	*ST*	*Non SC&ST*
Andhra Pradesh	58.4	51.5	65.1	41.5	41.4	52.7
Assam	76.0	100.0	84.9	73.0	86.4	78.5
Bihar	53.8	78.9	69.4	37.7	51.1	53.1
Gujarat	72.1	46.6	66.6	41.0	39.1	47.5
Haryana	52.2	37.5	66.5	32.2	70.7	43.1
Himachal Pradesh	65.0	100.0	66.0	61.4	80.1	71.3
Jammu & Kashmir	46.6	46.0	71.6	64.0	99.3	81.6
Karnataka	47.7	53.1	71.5	38.7	31.6	51.5
Kerala	72.0	74.0	81.3	59.3	52.7	80.4
Madhya Pradesh	50.8	55.8	62.7	27.3	24.0	35.9
Maharashtra	60.5	54.9	68.4	46.9	30.3	52.2
Orissa	53.4	47.0	70.9	39.3	32.1	55.0
Punjab	64.4	68.2	82.0	41.7	52.1	47.4
Rajasthan	65.9	53.4	73.8	49.6	42.8	62.8
Tamil Nadu	49.1	68.5	78.0	15.0	16.3	24.2
Uttar Pradesh	53.8	100.0	64.8	47.5	94.2	60.4
West Bengal	59.7	45.9	78.2	56.1	44.8	76.2
All-India	54.1	51.6	65.2	40.2	35.8	51.0

Source: NSSO Reports on Employment and Unemployment, 1997, 2001 and 2007.

The earning ratio of the workers is expected to follow the trend in their wage rate and thus, as the wage rates differ among the social groups, earning ratios too will differ among them. This will be particularly true in the case of those regions which are lagging behind in development, since the burden of backwardness will fall more heavily on the marginalised groups than on the advanced social groups in the society. The disparities among the social groups in the earnings ratio among the major states in 1999-2000 and 2005-06 indicate that the earning ratios of the workers belonging to SC and ST groups are certainly less than the earning ratio of the Non-SC&ST workers in both the time periods. Moreover, it is also the case with some of the advanced states like Maharashtra, Haryana and West Bengal. This suggests that social disparities in the earning ratios are quite pronounced not only in the backward states, but also in the advanced states, while it is moderate in those states which have achieved medium level of development. Hence, it can be said that there is a mixed trend as far as the regional disparities in the earning ratio among the social groups is concerned.

CONCLUSION

This analysis about the wage and employment conditions among the social groups during the post-reform period in India suggests that the situation is quite worse in both employment and wage among both SC and ST workforce as against the Non-SC&ST workforce. The degree of disparity among the social groups which was worsened between 1993-94 and 1999-2000, however has improved between 1999-2000 and 2005-06. In the era of globalisation, where the Government withdraws from the function of welfare state slowly, but steadily has put enormous pressure, especially on the marginalised groups, who are already living on the fringes of the society. Thus, it is not only necessary to provide the marginalised groups with more jobs through affirmative action like reservation, but also make them more employable with the help of high quality education and vocational training.

REFERENCES

Bhalla, A.S., and Lapeyre F., (1999), "Global Integration and Social Exclusion with Special Reference to Poland and Hungary, *European Journal of Development Research*, Vol. 11, No. 1.

Banerjee, B., and Knight, J.B., (1985), "Caste Discrimination in the Indian Labour Market", *Journal of Development Economics*, Vol. 17.

Borooah, Vani K., Dubey A., and Iyer S., (2005), "Has Job Reservation been Effective? Caste, Religion and Economic Status in India, Northern University of Ulster, November.

Duraisamy M., and Duraisamy P., (1996), "Sex Discrimination in Indian Labour Markets," *Feminist Economics*, Vol. 2, No. 2.

Govt. of India, "*Report on Employment and Unemployment in India*", NSSO, various reports.

Madheswaran S., and Lakshmanasamy T., (1996), "Occupational Segragation and Earnings Differentials by Sex: Evidence from India", *Artha Vijnana*, Vol. 38, No. 4.

Majumder, Rajarshi, (2009), "Earning Differentials Across Social Groups: Evidences from India", *MPRA Paper No. 12811*, January.

Nayak P., (1995), "Economic Development and Social Exclusion in India", in *Social Exclusion in South Asia*, ILO, Geneva.

Sundaram K., and Tendulkar S.D., (2003), "Poverty among Social and Economic Groups in India, in *India in the Nineteen Nineties,*, Working Paper No. 118.

11

SOCIO-ECONOMIC STUDY OF CHILD LABOUR IN OTTAPIDARAM TALUK TUTICORIN DISTRICT

D. AMUTHA & J. ELLORA

INTRODUCTION

Child hood is the blossoming period of a human being. A child has the right for everything that is enjoyed by an adult. Normally the children are physically and mentally unfit to work. But they are forced to join the work force due to many reasons. Despite hectic planning, welfare programmes, legislation and administrative action in the past five decades, a large majority of the Indian children continue to remain in distress.

The exploitation of children as labourers had led to various socioeconomic problems and it is one of the biggest problems in India. Generally the parents earn, look after and plan for the future of their children. But in poor families the children have to work and earn for their parents. In the study area namely Ottapidaram Taluk in Tuticorin District is taken as the field of experiment.

GLOBAL SCENARIO OF CHILD LABOUR

According to the International Labour Organization (ILO) Report (2000) 246 million child workers aged between 5 and 17 were involved in child labour of which 171 million were involved in work hazardous to their safety physical or mental health and moral development, the ILO publications (1998) indicate that the proportion of child labourers various a lot among countries and even among regions in those countries. 61% of child workers live in Asia, 32% in Africa, 7% in Latin America and 1% in the US, Canada, Europe and other wealthy nations. In Asia, 22% of the work force is children and in Latin America 17% of the workforce are children.

India

In India, according to 1991 census there were 11.29 million child workers. National sample survey figures for the year 1999-2000 indicated that there were 10.4 million child labourers.

Tamil Nadu

In Tamil Nadu, according to 2001 census, there are 81 lakhs child workers. 48.2% of them were male and 51.8% were female child workers. The survey conducted by Sarva Shiksha Abhiyan (SSA) in 2003 revealed that the number had dipped below one lakh and stood at 70,344 child labourers in Tamil Nadu.

Tuticorin District

The survey of child labour in Tuticorin District has identified 2655 child labourers. Of these 1491 are boys and 1164 are girls. Substantial number of child workers has been identified in Kovilpatti Municipality (125), Tuticorin Municipality (249), Kayathar (200), Kovilpatti Panchayat Union (339), Pudur (321) and Santhankulam (236). 460 children are in hazardous occupations. Among them 135 are boys and 325 are girls. It may be seen that girls outnumber boys. 2195 children are in non-hazardous occupation. Among them 1356 are boys and 839 are girls. 139 of the child labourers are aged less than 9 years. Among them 87 are boys and 52 are girls. 617 child labourers are in the age of 9-12. Of these, 347 are boys and 270 are girls. The largest number (1899) is in the age group of 12-14 years. Among them 1057 are boys and 842 are girls. The District Administration can admit children in the age group of 5-9 straight away to regular schools. Special schools are required for the children in the age group 9-14. Among the child labourers, 542 (20.4%) belong to SC, 1 (0.04%) belong to ST, 695 (26.2%) belong to MBC and 931 (35.1%) belong to BC. Only 486 (18.3%) children belong to other communities.

460 children are engaged in hazardous occupations. Among them the most prominent are Beedi making (31) and Manufacturing of matches (266). 2195 children are in non-hazardous occupation. Among non-hazardous occupations, the most prominent are coolie (101), sheep rearing (97), cattle grazing (38), shops and establishments (370), Fishing (168) and Catering establishment (47).

STATEMENT OF THE PROBLEM

The census report also reveals that child labour is more common in rural areas (about 91%) as compared to urban areas (about 9%). The problem of child labour in Tamil Nadu varies from district to district. The incidence of working girls is much higher than the working boys in almost all the districts of Tamil Nadu. In all the States as a whole, the working girls account for 7.06% and the boys account for 3.6% of the total working force. According to ILO classification a large proportion of children work in agriculture. More of girls are engaged in households while majority of boys work outside the households. The child labourers are made to work for hours together in a day. Normally they work for 10 to 12 hours per day. In course of time they would be subject to occupational diseases even during their childhood. Especially they are susceptible to mostly respiratory diseases such as chronic bronchitis and tuberculosis. Hence a study on child labour is needed and this paper makes an attempt on these aspects.

CAUSES OF CHILD LABOUR

Socio-economic conditions plays a significant role in giving rise to the problem of child labour. A variety of factors can be attributed for the employment of child workers. Some of them are

- Poverty is the single important reason for child labour
- Easy availability of child labour without many obligations for the employers,
- Many employers prefer to employ children because of cheap labour.
- Death of the earning member of the family
- Alcoholic and unemployed father in need of money for looking
- Ignorance and illiteracy of parents
- Lack of good schools and school drop-out
- Social structure and customs in the families, etc.

OBJECTIVES OF THE STUDY

- To understand the causes for child labour
- To analyse the income of the family and employment of children; and
- The health problems of child labourers.

HYPOTHESIS

There is no significant difference between the sex of the child workers and their parents' compulsion to do the works.

METHODOLOGY

The main purpose of the study is to have a critical view of the problems of the child worker. Thus the present study is based on primary data. There are approximately six hundred child workers in Ottapidaram Taluk. An individual child worker has been considered as a unit for the study. Therefore, 216 child workers engaged in various works were selected by stratified random sampling method. Moreover, not more than one child worker from the same family or house was considered. Among the 216 sample respondents 41 boys and 175 girls were selected. These workers are well versed in different works. The data then tabulated were systematically processed and interpreted on the basis of the objectives formulated. Most of the analyses were based on the relevant statistical tools such as percentages, averages and chi-square test.

Total number of SC families in the Ottapidaram Taluk is 810 out of which SC 216 families with children in the age group of 9 to 14 have been selected for this study. 62% of the child labour are employed in agriculture.

Two interesting findings during the field study are (i) Female population out number male population (ii) The population belonging to scheduled community is following Hindu religion. The data relates to the month of June 2009.

Population of Tuticorin and Ottapidaram Areas

		Population			*Schedule Caste*		
Block	*Area(sq.km)*	*Persons*	*Male*	*Female*	*Persons*	*Male*	*Female*
Tuticorin	366	405363	203368	201995	54364	27458	26906
Ottapidaram	738	114759	56989	57770	46495	23442	23053
		Literates			*Schedule Tribe*		
Tuticorin		309707	163647	146060	1107	562	545
Ottapidaram		76555	42328	34227	88	42	46

Source: 2001 census

RESULTS AND DISCUSSION

The sample of 216 child workers taken for this study consists of 175 girls (81.02 per cent) and 41 boys (18.98 per cent), all from the study area. Thus the sex distribution seems to be very much pronounced in this work. In the case of girls, parents feel that it is safe to stay at home with them while earning.

The table gives a picture on the educational background of the samples. One third of the parents are illiterates and 18% have been educated up to primary level. The study also revealed than in 115 families both the parents are illiterates. As most of the parents have low educational status, they do not have an aptitude to encourage their children to go for higher education.

Education of Parents

Level of Education	*Boys*	%	*Girls*	%	*Total*	%
Illiterate	21	9.72	94	43.52	115	53.24
Primary	8	3.70	31	14.35	39	18.05
Middle	6	2.78	26	12.04	32	14.82
Secondary	4	1.85	17	7.87	21	9.72
Higher Secondary	1	0.46	6	2.78	7	3.24
Graduation	1	0.46	1	0.46	2	0.92
Total	41	18.98	175	81.02	216	100.00

Source: Primary Data

The other factor which normally hinders the continuation of education is the number of children in the family. It is exciting to note that 192 families 89% out of 216 families have 3 and more children. A big question remains unanswered whether the population policy of the country has reached this sector. As the study is on the child dropout it requires an idea about the number of children in the family. So it is considered here.

Size of the Family

Family Size	*Boys*	%	*Girls*	%	*Total*	%
Below 3	6	2.78	18	8.33	24	11.11
3-5	13	6.02	54	25.00	67	31.02
5 and above	22	10.18	103	47.69	125	57.87
Total	41	18.98	175	81.02	216	100.00

Source: Primary Data

The drop-outs at the primary level is 53 percent and 37 percent at middle level and 10 percent at secondary level. The dropout rate is high at primary level.

Children Drop-outs

Drop out Stage	*Boys*	%	*Girls*	%	*Total*	%
Primary	24	11.11	90	41.67	114	52.78
Middle	13	6.02	67	31.02	80	37.04
Secondary	4	1.85	18	8.33	22	10.18
Total	41	18.98	175	81.02	216	100.00

Source: Primary Data

The main reason for child labour identified in this study is poverty and 60 percent child labour is due to poverty. The total 216 child workers, 58.80 per cent are compelled by their parents. The remaining 41.20 per cent have taken up the work after knowing by themselves of their family backwardness. Besides, the parents resort to employing their children in the work as they find no other alternative to earn money.

Reasons for Child Labour

Reasons	*Boys*	%	*Girls*	%	*Total*	%
Primary	24	11.11	90	41.67	114	52.78
Poverty	27	12.49	103	47.69	130	60.18
School drop-out	3	1.39	12	5.56	15	6.95
Big size of family	6	2.78	8	3.70	14	6.48
Low income	2	0.93	21	9.72	23	10.65
Illiteracy and ignorance of parents	3	1.39	31	14.35	34	15.74
Total	41	18.98	175	81.02	216	100.00

Source: Primary Data

HYPOTHESIS

There is no significant difference between the sex of the child workers and their parents' compulsion to do various works.

The testing of the hypothesis is based on the primary data collected from the study area. The Chi-square test has been applied to test the given hypothesis and the results are presented in the Table.

Observed Frequencies

Reasons	*Boys*	*Girls*	*Total*
Compulsion	28	99	127
No Compulsion	13	76	89
Total	41	175	216

Source: Primary Data

Since the calculated value of χ^2 (1.89) is less than the table value (3.84) this hypothesis is accepted. Therefore, we may conclude that there is no significant difference between the sex of the child workers and their parents' compulsion to do the works.

Employment of Child Labour

Occupation	*Boys*	%	*Girls*	%	*Total*	%
Fishing	1	0.46	–	–	1	0.46
Agriculture	12	5.56	103	47.69	115	53.24
Match industry	8	3.70	21	9.72	29	13.43
Beedi industry	14	6.48	40	18.52	54	25
Cattle grazing	3	1.39	4	1.85	7	3.24
Plantations	3	1.39	7	3.24	10	4.63
Total	41	18.98	175	81.02	216	100.00

Source: Primary Data.

The table reveals that 38.43% of the child labour is employed in match and beedi industries and 61.57% are employed in agriculture.

EARNING OF CHILD WORKERS

The Table reveal that, 13.42 per cent of child workers earn income upto Rs.300 to 500; 70.37 per cent of them earn Rs.500 to 700; 10.69 per cent of them earn Rs.700 to 900 and 5.52 per cent of them earn Rs.900 to 1,100. The average monthly income of boys is Rs.643.90 and that of girls is Rs.610.29. Their combined average monthly income is Rs.616.67. The analysis of data shows that the earning of boys is more than the earning of girls. The reason is that the parents compel their boy children to confine themselves to various works.

Earnings per month of the Respondents

Amount (in Rs)	*Boys*		*Girls*		*Total*	
	No.	*%*	*No.*	*%*	*No.*	*%*
Rs.300-500	10	4.63	19	8.79	29	13.42
Rs.500-700	17	7.87	135	62.58	152	70.37
Rs.700-900	9	4.17	14	6.48	23	10.65
Rs.900-1,100	5	2.31	7	3.24	12	5.52
Total	41	18.98	175	81.02	216	100.00

Source: Primary Data

HOUSEHOLD INCOME

The household income in the present study consists of all the members of the family including the respondent child worker. The classification of households according to their monthly income is shown in the Table.

Household Income of the Respondents Family

Monthly Income (in Rs)	*No of Respondents*	*Percentage*
1,000 - 1,500	26	12.04
1,500 - 2,000	58	26.85
2,000 - 2,500	90	41.67
2,500 - 3,000	22	10.19
3,000 - 3,500	8	3.70
3,500 - 4,000	12	5.56
Total	216	100.00

Source: Primary Data

It is clear from the above table that 41.67 per cent of the households fall under the income category of Rs.2,000 to 2,500. About 3.70 per cent of households come under the income category Rs.3,000 to 3,500 and only 5.56 per cent of them are in the higher income category of Rs.3,500 to 4,000. The analysis shows that the average monthly income of the households is Rs.2166.67.

OCCUPATIONAL DISEASES

The child workers are deprived of their right to be care-free as children and their right to education. The burden of work causes various types of health problems especially back pain, fever, headache, dysentery etc. These diseases affect them physically and mentally.

It is clear from the above data that the child workers are affected by more than one disease at a particular time. It is observed that a great majority (91.02 per cent) of the children are reported to have body and back pains. Besides, about 82.64 per cent of the children are subjected to fever. 80.85 per cent of the children are subjected to frequent cold and cough and 94.61 percent of the children are subjected to headache.

Types of Occupational Diseases

Kinds of Diseases	*Boys*			*Girls*			*Grand*
	Yes	*No*	*Total*	*Yes*	*No*	*Total*	*Total*
Frequent cold & cough	23 (13.77)	5 (2.99)	28 (16.77)	112 (67.08)	27 (16.17)	139 (83.23)	167 (100)
Headache	26 (15.57)	2 (1.20)	28 (16.77)	132 (79.04)	7 (4.19)	139 (83.23)	167 (100)
Fever	20 (11.98)	8 (4.79)	28 (16.77)	118 (70.66)	21 (12.57)	139 (83.23)	167 (100)
Back pain & Body pain	23 (13.77)	5 (2.99)	28 (16.77)	129 (77.25)	10 (5.99)	139 (83.23)	167 (100)
Dysentery	21 (12.57)	7 (4.19)	28 (16.77)	14 (8.38)	125 (74.85)	139 (83.23)	167 (100)
Chromic Bronchitis	7 (4.19)	21 (12.57)	28 (16.77)	9 (5.39)	130 (77.84)	139 (83.23)	167 (100)

Note: Figures in Parentheses indicate percentages

FINDINGS

The main findings of the present study are summarised below:

The study discloses that 81.02 per cent of child labourers employed in various works in the study area are girls. The proportion of the working girls is many times more than that of the boys. The study discloses, that 58.80 per cent of children are compelled by their parents to take up various works. It is also proved by (χ^2) Chi-square test that parents have compelled their children to take up various works irrespective of their sex due to poverty. The study shows that the average monthly income of boys 643.90 is more than the average monthly income of girls 610.29. The analysis of the data shows that the average monthly income of the households is Rs. 2166.67. The study shows that 91.92 per cent of the children are reported to have body and back pains.

SUGGESTIONS

- The poverty eradication programmes like IRDP, NREP and RIEGP are to be intensified to raise the income level of the parents. This is to obviate the economic needs of these families to send the young ones to work.
- The minimum wage Act should be strictly enforced to raise the income level of the parents.
- Wide adult literacy compulsion should be conducted to make the parents more education conscious.
- Parents should be complied through legislative enactments to educate their children up to a certain age
- The parents should be advised to limit the size of their family by adopting family planning methods

- The parents should be compensated for their economic loss, while sending their children to school.

CONCLUSION

Inspite of the government measures and incentives, the child labour can not be eradicated completely unless the society especially the parent cooperate with the government. The parents must be willing to discharge their duties and responsibilities towards their children. The parents should feel ashamed of getting income through their children.

REFERENCES

Prasad, T., "Preventing Exploitation of Children", *Social Welfare,* Vol. 29, No. 5, August 1982, p. 35.

Smiths Kothari, "Child Labour in Sivakasi", *Economic and Political Weekly,* 2, July, 1983, p. 119.

ILO: *Child Labour: Targeting the Intolerable* (Geneva, 1996).

Weiner Myron (1991), "The Child and The State in India," OUP.

Karunanithi, "Child Labour in Beedi Industries", p. 50.

A.N. Sadu and Amerjit Singh, "Child Labour in India", *The Indian Worker,* 29: October 1980, p. 61.

Smiths Kothari, "Child Labour in Sivakasi", *Economic and Political Weekly,* 2 July, 1983, p. 119.

12

SOCIAL TRANSFORMATION: AN ETHNOGRAPHIC EXPLORATION OF MALAYALIS, YELAGIRI HILLS, TAMIL NADU

L. KATHIRESAN

INTRODUCTION

An attempt was made to understand the process of social transformation of Malayalis[1] in Yelagiri hills, Vellore District, Tamil Nadu. By social transformation I mean those changes in their values, customs, traditions, social, economic, juridio-political, and cultural practices[2], etc.

Tribes in India constituting about 8 per cent of the total population had been subjected to oppression and exploitation for several years even after independence. Tribes in India have been facing numerous social and economic problems such a poverty, hunger, unemployment, exploitation, illiteracy, inequality, discrimination, remoteness, exclusion, deprivation, poor sanitation, unsafe drinking water, etc.

After Independence, tribal development is given national importance. Directive Principles of State Policy suggest that the government shall promote with special care the educational and economic interests of tribals and protect them from all forms of exploitation. Tribal situation in India is unique and extensive. It requires a care and special consideration in planning and implementing programmes and schemes for tribal population.

Various legislative, administrative and developmental measures are introduced. Constitutional safeguard and social legislation protected the rights of tribal people. However, land hungry non-tribals and moneylenders alienated the tribals from their land. Rights over forest and forest produce still remains controversial. Oppression and exploitation never come to an end.

National Commission for Scheduled Tribe was established to investigate and monitor matters relating to the constitutional safeguards, protect the rights of tribals, and, recommend, monitor and evaluate the effective implementation of socio-economic development measures by the governments. It is debatable whether tribals are emancipated or not. Basic infrastructural facilities are yet to reach tribal pockets.

Programmes such as, community development programmes, multi-purpose tribal development schemes, integrated tribal development projects, 20 point programmes with special reference to tribals, integrated rural development programmes, tribal sub-plans and hill area development porgrammes are introduced to uplift the tribals. Several nongovernmental organizations have also actively involved in tribal development activities. However, the status of tribals has not changed remarkably.

In this backdrop, this chapter demonstrates the process of social transformation of Malayalis in Yelagiri Hills.

YELAGIRI HILLS

Yelagiri hills are located in Eastern Ghats, 213 kilometres south west of Chennai, 91 kilometres from Vellore the district headquarter and 18 kilometres from Jollarpettai, of which 14 kilometres are mountain road having 14 hairpin bends, with few mountain viewpoints. Each bend is named after the great Tamil scholars and patrons as Paavender, Bharathiyar, Thiruvalluver, Elango, Kambar, Kabilar, Avvaiyar, Paari, Kaari, Ori, Aayi, Athiyamaan, Nalli, and Pegan. The weather in winter in Yelagiri is 11° C and in summer 34° C, which is considered to be the coolest in the district. The average rainfall is 900 mm. Yelagiri in its forest has number of flora and fauna some of which are considered as the rare. Yelagiri Hills occupies area of 29.2 sq kilometres.

Yelagiri was declared as the tourists spot in 1984 by the government of Tamil Nadu. Since then, various development initiatives had been undertaken and several places of interest were set up. In Poonganoor, a Lake was constructed for purpose of tourism occupying area of 56,706 sq meters with capacity of 4.86 million sq ft water. The depth of the lake is between 10 to 20 meters. A concrete road around the lake was build to facilitate the tourists to move around the lake. Different species of fish is farmed and sold to the tourists. In the centre of the lake a colourful artificial fountain is constructed to beautify the lake. A Children Park is constructed nearer to the lake covering area of six acres having lawns, trees, paths, playgrounds, picnic areas and other facilities for recreational and relaxation. The Park also has a mini zoo, which is maintained by Forest Department, Tirupattur. The Department also owns a nursery where rare species of *Siddha* and *Ayurvedha* herbal plants are cultivated. Lord Murugan Temple is another centre of attraction closer to which a community hall is built to conduct public meetings, marriage and other festivals. A Telescopic Centre in the thirteenth hairpin bend of the mountain road is setup by the forest department, Tirupattur, at an altitude of 1000 meters. Temple of Yelagiri Tamilannai is constructed in the seventh hairpin bend. The tourists, vehicle drivers and the tribes perform Pooja for Goddess of Tamil, Lord Ganesha and Anumaan.

Swami Malai, near Village Mangalam, is the highest hilltop in Yelagiri. Evidences of early civilization are found and preserved here. Mountain caves, Matheswaran trekking point, sun set and sun rise viewpoints, bird eye view of Kavalur Telescopic Centre and the plain land of Jawadhi rang are some other interested places. Jalagampaarai water falls, temples of Nilavoor, hotels and restaurants, guesthouses, residential schools and other educational institutions, weekly market, forest fruits and other minor produces, summer festival, and *paran* house are other centre of attraction in the hills.

Yelagiri is a Panchayat comprising fourteen villages namely, Muthanoor, Kottaiyur, Poonganoor, Athanavoor, Kottoor, Pallakanivoor, Mettukanivoor, Nilavoor, Rayaneri, Paaduvanoor, Putthur, Thaayaloor, Mangalam and Manchankolli Pudhur. This Panchayat is administratively functioning under Jollarpettai Block and Tirupattur Taluk. Malayalis are the only predominant scheduled tribe inhabits in this hilly region. The tourists interests created here has exposed Malayalis to the mainstream population and induced Malayalis for socio-cultural changes.

THE ORIGIN

There are numerous oral traditions about the origin of Malayalis. Colonial writers (Cox, 1881; Fancis, 1906; Thuston, 1909) provide a detail description on this account. Arthur F. Cox writes,

> In S.S. 1055 (A.D.1132) some of the Vedars of Kangundi asked that wives should be given them by the Kondekatti Vellalas of Cojeeveram. They were scornfully refused, and in anger kidnapped seven young Vellala maidens, whom they carried away to Kangundi. To recover them seven Vellala men set out, with seven dogs, leaving instructions with their wives that if the dogs retuned alone they should consider that they had perished, and should cause their funeral ceremonies to be performed. Arrived at the Palar, they found that river in flood and crossed it with difficulty; but their dogs, after swimming half way, turned back and returned to Conjeeveram. These men, however, continued their journey and killed the Vedars who had taken away their maidens, after which they went back to their homes, but found that they had been given up as lost, their wives had become widows, their funeral ceremonies performed, and they were in consequence outcastes. Under these circumstances, they contracted marriages with some Vedar women and retired to the Jewadis by way of Arni and Padaved, where they took to cultivation and become the ancestors of the Malayali caste (Cox, 1881).

Another colonial writer H. Le Fanu gives a different account on the origin of Malayali tribes. According to him, Malayali tribes are originally belonged to the Vellala caste of cultivators from Kanchipuram. Three brothers migrated to these hills about ten generations ago. Of whom the eldest came to the Shevaroy hills, the second to the Kolli hills, and the youngest to the Pachaimalai (green hills). According to another version of story, he writes,

> The Malaialis deity Kariraman, finding himself uncomfortable at Kanchi, took up a new abode. Three of his followers, named Periyanan, Naduvanan, and Chinnanan (the eldest, the middle-man, and the youngest) started with their families to follow him from Kanchi, and came to the Salem district, where they took different routes, Periyanan going to the Shevaroys, Naduvannan to the Pachamalais and Anjur hills, and Chinnan to Manjavadi (Fanue, 1883).

But F. J. Richard in his District Gazetteers gives an account, which is stated below.

> The legend runs that three brothers, by name Periyannan, Naduvannan and Chinnannan, went a hunting in a forest accompanied by three hunting hounds, and it came on to rain so heavily for two days that they were not able to quit the forest. Their hounds, however, returned home, and their wives, seeing the dogs without their masters, concluded that their husbands had died in the jungles, and accordingly, as all loyal widows should do, set fire to their houses and perished in the flames. On the third day the hunters returned to find their houses in ashes and their wives dead. The bereaved husbands thereupon consoled themselves by marrying again; Periyannan chose a Kaikolar girl, and settled on the Kalrayans; Naduvannan chose a Vedacbi as his bride, and the Pachai-malais as his residence; Chinnannan married a Devendra Pallan, and made his home on the Kolli-malais. These three brothers thus became the progenitors of the three clearly defined sub-castes into which the Malaiyalis are divided, the Periya-Malaiyalis, tlie Pachai-Malaiyalis and the Kolli-Malaiyalis (Richards, 1918).

Similar description is also given by F. R Hemingway about the legendary origin of the Malayalis of Trichy. Another story of betrayal depicts how the *Vellalas* married to the *Vedas* women.

> Once, the army of the king who ruled from Kancheepuram was defeated by a Muslim invader. A group of soldiers from this defeated army found shelter in the Kalrayan hills. The innocent tribals (Vedars) gave food and shelter to them. But after a while these soldiers felt restless. They couldn't go back to their families as the Muslim ruler fixed price for their heads. So they hatched out a plot. They invited all the males of the tribals for a grand farewell feast, saying that they are planning to go back. In this dinner all the male tribals were killed by the plot and their wives and daughters were taken captives by the soldiers (oral tradition).

As a sign of this betrayal, a gunshot is still heard during the marriage ceremony. It is also said that Krishna Devaraya of the Vijayanagar Empire was once helped by certain tribal families in this area and thus got a Charter from him to levy taxes which gave rise to the *jagirdari* system.

Though, these myths and legends resemble like fairy tales, people have strong faith at their deepest level in believing these stories and performing rituals. Malayalis of Yelagiri thus believe that they are from Kanchipuram and call themselves as *Goundar/Vellala Goundar*. The following section outlines social organisations of Malayalis.

SOCIAL ORGANISATION

The basic unit of Malayali social organisation is family which forms the Malayali kinship. Malayalis live in *kudumbangal/Veedu* (families). Recruitment of members is usually is done through marriages which are patrilocal in nature. These Patrilineal families are usually headed by males. Hierarchy in the family is based on the biological factors such as age and sex.

Malayalis traditionally lived in joint family. Due to various factors, the traditional joint families are splitting into nuclear families. As a result only a few families are sustaining with the joint family structure. Most of the informants have expressed that partition after marriage is better than living jointly with hard feelings. However, siblings and parents always extent their full cooperation and support to the young couples not only in setting up their families but also in their economic activities. Even though land is divided, they all work together. If the young parents migrate out in search of seasonal employment, during that period, their children are taken care by their paternal uncles or by their grandparents. This condition creates another change in the structure of the families *i.e.* extended families. However, their number is very less.

Malayalis are divided into number of exogamous *kudumbangal* that are equal in status. *Kudumbangal* are named based on their *Kula Deivam* (family deity) *i.e.*, Poonganura, Mangalathamaba and Kottoorama. Cross cousin marriage is the most common marriage pattern among Malayalis. At present, the age at marriage for boys is around twenty years while girls get married after attaining puberty.

Spouses are acquired through trial in the past, in which the prospective groom will stay in bride's family before marriage. If they like each other and then the elder would arrange the marriage. Earlier there was a practice in which the girl should become pregnant before the marriage and show the person who made her pregnant. Then they will get married. At present, the marriages are generally done through negotiations, elopement and courtship.

The marriage rituals are performed as it is done in the Hindu marriage. But it is not performed through a Brahmin but by the local *poosari*. Marriage oath is taken on *samai or ragi* by both bride and groom. Marriage is conducted in the groom's house. Traditionally, the ceremony lasted for five days but it is now reduced to two days. The groom hosts two feasts in which pork is a compulsory item in the menu. Depending upon the economic conditions and social status the feast is given. In addition, the groom will give clothes to his relatives. If he is rich enough, he will give cloths to all the invitees. There will be a procession of newly married couple in *mandai* (a common place mostly used during festival season). During the procession, the couple will get blessings from the villagers. The couple has to kneel down to everyone irrespective of their age. The couple accepts gifts from the marriage invitees. Generally, jewels are given as gifts. The value varies according to closeness of the invitees. This jewels become one of the valuable assets for the couple and in time of need it is pledged for loan in Tirupattur.

Sanskritization[3] has been attracting the rich people of Malayalis. This has influenced their traditional practices. A few instances are reported that their marriages rituals have been performed by Brahmin and which were entirely different from the traditional marriages. Presently, Malayalis have started to give Sanskrit names to their off-springs as against the traditionally given Tamil names.

Parayam (bride price) and *voor kattu* (marriage fee paid to the village) is paid at the time of marriage both in cash and kind by groom. *Parayam* is given to the bride family traditionally it was a meagre amount. But, as they came in contact with the general population, the amount of bride price has been increased gradually. At present, paying the bride price has become a customary practice; instead, dowry has been collected from the bride family by the groom family.

Divorce is allowed. If the man claims divorce the man has to pay compensation to the female and an amount as *voor kattu* to the village. Generally, this is determined by the bargaining capacity of the groom. Similarly, if a female claims divorce she has to pay back the *pariyam* that was paid by the groom to her family at the time of their marriage.

POLITICAL SYSTEM

Village is called as *voor* (village) and approximately thirty to fifty families constitute a *voor*. A *voor* is administered by a village council. All the families in a particular settlement are the member of the council. *Voor Gounder* (village leader), *Udtheri* and *Poosari* are the office bearers of the council. They execute its functions in consultation with its members. The council will meet in a common place called *Jawadi*. The council will decide on all the matters concerning the village and its people. Any personal or public issue which needs the council's recognition or help will be brought to the notice of *Voor Gounder*.

By the order of *Voor Gounder, Udtheri* (messenger) will inform the villages and ask them to assemble at *Jawadi*. *Voor Gounder* and other important elder will set on the stage of *Jawadi*. *Voor Gounder* will wear *thalai paagai* (head covering) while he starts *Panchayat* (village meeting). This is also known as *mudi kattu*. The petitioners and the respondents have to stand when they are asked to report or answer. After hearing both the parties, *Voor Gounder* will seek public opinion. Sometimes a jury will be formed to investigate the issue if another *voor* is involved. All the members are free to suggest the council or to resolve to arrive at a solution. However, finally the *naayam* (verdict) is declared by *Voor Gounder*. If guilty is proved, the cow-down is applied on the criminal's head. Later this punishment is given with fine. The council had dealt all the matters in the past such as marriage, separation, crime, village festivals, public works etc. The entry of police, judicial administration and Panchayat Raj has limited the scope of the traditional village council. At present, the council deals with conjugal matters and the disputes that can be settled at the village level

Traditionally, if the dispute is not amicably settled at the *Voor Panchayat the* matter will be referred to *naatar*, who is the tribal leader of a *Nadu*. Ten to fifteen *voor* constitute a *nadu*. Yelagiri *nadu* comprises fourteen villages. The role of *naatar* is to settle any dispute that arises between *voors*. He is assisted by a person called *manthiri* (minister). Both of them are elected unanimously by the people and communicated to other *nadugal* (plural of *nadu*). *Naatar* will call the village representatives with *voor goundergal* (plural of *gounder)* of both disputed villages and negotiate with them to settle the issue. If the dispute is not settled at this stage, or at any inter *nadu*, disputes will be taken by Ezhu-*Pattu nadugal* which are (1) Yelagiri Malai, (2) Jawadhi Malai, (3) Pongam Pattu Nadu, (4) Pudhur Nadu, (5) Nelli Vasal Nadu, (6) Jamanamattur Nadu, (7) Themmalai Nadu, (8) Chitteri Nadu, (9) Kolli Malai and (10) Kavarayan Nadu. All the *naatar* and their ministers and *voor goundergal* will be called for meeting of Ezhu-*Pattu nadugal*. However, the modern political and judicial systems have replaced the traditional systems of Malayalis which also become week and incompetent to deal with the modern law and order problem.

ECONOMIC SYSTEM

Agriculture is the principal occupation in Yelagiri Hills. Out of 4689.86 acres of registered land, 3556.2 acres of dry and 338.8 acres of wet lands available for cultivation in the Yelagiri (and the remaining land is not used for agricultural purpose). They cultivate cereals such as paddy, ragi, *solam, makka solam, pani varagu, samai* and *thinnai*; pulses like *thuvarai, avarai, vulundhu* and *kollu*; cash corps like pepper, mustard, sugarcane, plantain, *yellu, daniya* and *kadukaai*; and vegetables such as, tomato, beans, jackfruit, lady's finger, drum-stick, brinjal, etc.

Traditionally, the agricultural activities are carried out through *Voor Kambalam*. That is, the employer will inform the *gounder* about the need of labour. This message will be communicated to all families by *uddari*. One person from each family will undertake the job. Male or female *Kambalam* is called by the needy depending upon the work. This type of employment ranges from half a day *kambalam* to till the work gets over. The practice of *kambalam* is flexible to meet the labour requirement and to provide equal employment opportunity to all the families. The nature of work available through *kambalam* are ploughing, sowing, weeding, harvesting, transporting the harvest from land to home, etc. Male is paid Rs. 25 and Rs. 20 to females per day with a noon meals as an honorarium. Generally, *samai choru* or *nellu choru* (rice) with *sambhar* is offered depending upon the economic status of the employer. *Nellu choru* is considered to be rich. But, nowadays, this menu is increased with *vadaa* or a sweet. Another notable change in the *voor kambalam* is *siru wardu kambalam*. As the difference of opinion came between *kudumbangal* they stopped calling *voor kambalam.* Instead the *kambalam* is shared among relatives exclusively.

The tribal villages, the *nadu* and *voor* were governed by the tribal leaders, *natar* and *voor gounder* respectively. Before the introduction of *patta* system (individual landholding right), the agricultural land was the community property. So the leader would allocate the land to each family for cultivation every year considering the family size and its requirements. However, the leader would get more land than others. During the harvesting season, each family would deposit the grains in a common place under the custody of *voor gounder* as the measure of food security in case of monsoon failures in the forthcoming seasons. Whenever, there is a need the community will share the grains. In case if the common grain is exhausted the *gounder* would distribute his grains. In case of drought he and his *voor* representatives would seek help from *natar*. Besides the food security, the accumulated food grains had been used for the village festivals and tribal marriages. But after the *patta* system, the means of production is no more under community control. As a result, the practice of accumulating the grains in one place got vanished. For the purpose of festivals and marriage, the village council would fix the quantity to be deposited. Similarly, a deposit for seed is also collected and store in a safe common place as to prevent the seed scarcity. So the community deposit has changed from voluntary to forced deposit and from food security to seed security. At present people stopped even storing seeds as the hi-breed seeds are supplied through Large scale Adivasi Multipurpose Societies (LAMPS) by the government.

Besides agriculture, a large number of people earn their livelihood through gathering minor forest produce. Historically, even after settled agriculture, Malayalis were dependent on minor forest produce. They used to collect *moongil arisi* (bamboo rice), *theyen* (honey), *kizhangu* (yam), fruits, *puli* (tamarind), *kadukaai, dhandikaai, vasanai pul, manam pul, pungan, veppam,* amla, *seekakaai,* firewood and timber, etc. In the past, they collected the forest minor produce for their own consumption, and later they collected them to sell in the market in plains to buy cloths, jaggery, oil, kerosene and salt. As the demand increased, intermediates came into Yelagiri and they started exploiting the tribe by paying them less. The access to the forest is denied to Malayalis as the government declared it as reserved. Cutting of trees for timber and collection of firewood, for sale has been completely stopped. Consequently, people who lived depending on forest were force to violate the rules. This has become an advantage to the intermediates to exploit them severely.

Besides these, the tourism related development had provided some opportunity for a small population. Forest department and *Gram Panchayat* offer some seasonal employment. However, vast unemployment and huge land alienation forced the people to find more jobs in the neighbouring towns. The formation of SEM *magalir mandram* (Women Self Help Groups) by Centre for Rural Health and Social Education (CRHSE) is a phenomenal achievement which brought out the entrepreneur skills of female Malayalis.

CONCLUSION

Traditional Malayali society once lived in isolation. The introduction of tourism and development initiates brought them to expose to change and to the general population. Also, the in-build potentials for change have brought drastic change in their social institutions. Traditional joint families are breaking into nuclear small families. Proselytisation diminishes their cultural and ritual values. Changes in the political institutions made the traditional system incompatible to the modern life. Varied employment opportunities created a high economic differentiation among Malayali community. In this context, elite groups and associations work to preserve the Malayali cultural identities.

NOTES

1. Malayalis is ethnic group from Tamil Nadu, constitutionally categorized as Scheduled Tribe. Malayalis is a Tamil word to denote hill dwellers (malai = hill, ali = dweller) and it does not mean Malayalam speaking people from Kerala.
2. It is a multi dimensional concept. It denotes the long term socio-cultural changes 'in response to such factors as economic growth, war or political upheavals' (Castles, 2001). To contrast it from social change, social transformation does not have any pre-determined goal such as upward mobility within a particular community. Social transformation may not be positive all the time, for example loosing identity.
3. In 1952, M. N. Srinivas first introduced the notion of Sanskritization in his book "Religion and Society among the Coorg". He defines it as process of positional change by which a low caste or a tribal group changes its customs, rituals, ideology and way of life in the direction of a high caste.

REFERENCES

Castles, S. (2001), Studying Social Transformation. *International Political Science Review*, 22 (1), 13-32.

Cox, A. F. (1881), A Manual of the North Arcot District in the Presidency of Madras. Chennai: Tamilnadu Achieves, Government of Tamilnadu.

Department of Tourism, (2002), VELLORE ELAGIRI Tamil Nadu - India (Pamphlet), Chennai: Government of Tamil Nadu.

Fancis, W. (1906), Madras District Gazetteers: South Arcot. Madras: The Superintendent, Government Press.

Fanue, H. L. (1883), A Manual of the Salem District in the Presidency of Madras. Chennai: Tamilnadu Achieves, Government of Tamilnadu.

Richards, F. J. (1918), Madras District Gazetteers: Salem Vol. I - Part. I. Madras: The Superintendent, Government Press.

Srinivas, M. N. (1952), Religion and Society among the Coorgs of South India. Asia Publishing House: Bombay.

13

MICRO FINANCE: SHG – BANK LINKAGE PROGRAMME

C. DHANDAPANI

INTRODUCTION

Micro finance has gained significance and momentum from the last decade. India now occupies a significant place and a niche in global micro finance through promotion of the Self -Help Groups and the home grown SHG-Bank Linkage model. The Indian model offers promise and potential to address poverty as it is focused on building social capital through providing access to financial services.

In the words of Nobel Peace Prize winner for the year 2006 Muhammad Yunus "lasting peace cannot be achieved unless large population groups find ways in which to break out of poverty. Micro credit is one such means. Development from below also serves to advance democracy and human rights". Hence, the new concept micro finance emerged with Self-Help Groups.

DEFINITION OF MICRO FINANCE

Micro finance means providing the credit facilities to the rural and urban poor, especially women to start business, invest in self employment works so as to increase their income and standard of living. It is the extension of small loans to poor who have no employment.

The declaration of the Micro Credit Summit, held in Washington DC in 1977, defined micro credit programmes as those 'extending small loans to poor people for self- employment projects that generate income, allowing them to care for themselves and their families'. In India, the Task Force on Supportive and Regulatory Framework for Micro Finance defined microfinance as the 'provision of thrift, credit and other financial services and products of very small amounts to the poor in rural, semi-urban or urban areas enabling them to raise their income levels and improve living standards'.

In India, 75 million households depend on money lenders for their financial needs. Almost 90 percent of the rural people have no access to insurance. Poverty and unemployment have been permanent problems since independence, especially, in rural areas. Governments have been implementing several programmes like Integrated Rural Development Programme (IRDP) in rural areas. But these programmes have not yielded desired results due to low participation of rural masses. Micro finance was considered as a crucial one in the rural reconstruction. Micro finance can be a large scale poverty alleviation tool which can uplift the standard of living of the poorest of the poor.

EVOLUTION OF MICRO FINANCE IN INDIA

In Gujarat, in 1974, Self Employed Woman's Association (SEWA), a small trade group of woman, was established on cooperative principles. This NGO provided banking services to the poor and self employed women working as venders, hawkers, and domestic servants etc., who are employed in the unorganized sector in Ahmadabad. This was the beginning of Self-Help Group movement in India. Working Women's Forum (WWF) has started promoting working women's co-operative societies in Tamil Nadu since 1980. Shreyas in Kerala actively involved in the micro finance operation since 1988 with the objective of promoting people's cooperatives.

A self help group comprises individuals who voluntarily save small amounts of money in a common pool, from which need based loans are given to the members to meet their credit needs based on priority. In other words, a SHG can be referred as a group of poor people, who own, manage and control a micro bank of their own. The aim of SHG is to fight poverty through self confidence, solidarity and social security to control and guide their destinies.

MODELS OF MICRO FINANCE SERVICES

Various Commercial Banks, Cooperative Banks and Regional Rural Banks are involved in delivering micro finance. These banks further categorized into three models. They are: (1) Banks provide micro finance to Non-Governmental Organizations (NGOs) for on- lending to the Self Help Groups (SHGs) and ultimately to the small entrepreneurs, (2) Banks provide direct financing to SHGs for on-lending to the small entrepreneurs, (3) Banks finance directly to SHGs for on-lending to small entrepreneurs, with the intervention of NGOs and social organizations.

FEATURES OF MICRO FINANCE

The micro credits are small loans given to poor households in rural and urban areas for income generation through self-employment. Micro credit institutions also provide facilities for savings and other financial services.

The following are some of the features of micro credit: (1) Micro finance gives loans without collateral security. (2) The NABARD Task Force identifies three ways of banking with the poor: a) by means of conventional bank lending, (b) linking SHGs with bank lending, and (c) bank lending to micro credit and micro finance institutions for on- lending to groups or individuals. The second and third methods are characterized by low transactions costs and high repayments. (3) Micro credit is viewed as a way of promoting market led growth or in the words of Mohammed Yunus, of 'privatizing the economy. (4) The main target group of micro credit is the people who are living below the line of poverty. (5) The NABARD Task Force estimated the credit requirement per family as Rs. 6000 in rural areas and Rs.9000 in urban areas and it recommended that the average loan given to members of SHGs be around Rs. 1000. The micro credit cell of RBI, however, has proposed a ceiling of Rs. 25 000 for micro finance, and suggests that the ceiling may be increased to Rs. 40 000.

MICRO FINANCE-SHG - BANK LINKAGE PROGRAMME

The SHG-Bank Linkage Programme of NABARD has emerged as the Primary model for providing Micro-Finance (MF) services in the country. It is a proven tool of extending to the unbanked rural clientele access to formal financial services. For the success of the programme, NABARD promoted the linkage of Micro- Finance Institutions (MFIs) with the banking sector. The MFI–Bank Linkage model also has assumed importance on account of credit support extended by banks for on-lending to clients by MFIs.

PROGRESS OF SHG-BANK LINKAGE PROGRAMME

A significant expansion of the programme was witnessed during 2004-05 with a credit linkage of 5, 39,385 new SHGs by the banking system indicating growth of 49 per cent over the previous year. The cumulative number of SHGs credit linked increased to 16.18 lakhs while the bank loan extended increased to Rs.6, 898.46 crores as on 31 March 2005. The United Nations has designated the year 2005 as the 'International Year of Micro Credit'.

As on March 31, 2006, 29.24 lakhs SHGs in 587 district of the country have been credit- linked to 44,500 branches of 50 commercial banks, 352 cooperative banks and96 Regional Rural Banking (RRBs). The cumulative credit, which has flown to these groups, is Rs 18,040.74 crores and the cumulative refinance drawn from NABARD is to the extent of Rs 5,446.49 crores.

During the year 2007-08, 5,52,992 new SHGs (excluding SGSY) were credit linked with banks and bank loan of Rs.2,541.98 crores disbursed, taking the cumulative number of SHGs credit linked to 34,77,965 as on 31 March 2008. In addition 1, 86,883 existing SHGs were provided repeat loan of Rs.1, 685.60 crores.

As on 31 March 2007, 41.60 lakhs SHGs maintained savings and had savings of Rs.3, 512.71 crores outstanding with the banking sector. The programme has covered more than 5.8 crores poor households, making it the largest micro finance programme in the world. During 2006-07, bank credit of Rs.6, 570.39 crores and Rs.1, 151.56 crores were disbursed to 11.05 lakhs SHGs (including 1.88 lakhs under SGSY) and 334 MFIs, respectively. The overall progress of the micro finance programme is given in the Table 1 below.

Table 1
Cumulative Growth in SHG-Bank Linkage -As on 31 March

(*Figures in Numbers*)

S.No	*Priority State*	*2002*	*2003*	*2004*	*2005*	*2006*	*2007*
1	Assam	1,024	3,477	10,706	31,234	56,499	81,454
2	Bihar	3,957	8,161	16,246	28,015	46,221	72,339
3	Chhattisgarh	3,763	6,763	9,796	18,569	31,291	41,703
4	Gujarat	9,496	13,875	15,974	24,712	34,160	43,572
5	Himachal Pradesh	5,069	8,875	13,228	17,798	22,920	27,799
6	Jharkhand	4,198	7,765	12,647	21,531	30,819	37,317
7	Maharashtra	19,619	28,065	38,535	71,146	1,31,470	2,25,856
8	Madhya Pradesh	7,981	15,271	27,095	45,105	57,125	70,912
9	Orissa	20,553	42,272	77,588	1,23,256	1,80,896	2,34,451
10	Rajasthan	12,564	22,742	33,846	60,006	98,171	1,37,837
11	Uttar Pradesh	33,114	53,696	79,210	1,19,648	1,61,911	1,98,587
12	Uttarakhand	3,323	5,853	10,908	14,043.	17,588	21,527
13	West Bengal	17,143	32,647	51,685	92,698	1,36,251	1,81,563
	Total	1,41,804	2,49,462	3,97,464	6,67,761	10,05,272	13,74,917

Source: Annual Report of NABARD 2007-2008, Mumbai.

In order to reduce the regional imbalances in the spread of the SHG-Bank Linkage Programme, NABARD identified 13 States which have a large population of the poor, for focused attention. The cumulative number of SHGs credit linked in these 13 states increased from 10.05 lakhs in 2005-06 to 13.75 lakhs in 2006-07. During 2006-07, the number of SHGs credit linked in 13 priority states constituted 53.9 per cent in the all India credit linkage of 6,86,408 SHGs. As on 31 March 2008, an amount of Rs.2, 541.04 lakhs was released and 1.75 lakhs SHGs credit linked to banks.

MICRO CREDIT IN TAMIL NADU

In Tamil Nadu, 86,166 new SHGs were credit linked during 2006-07 and the cumulative number of SHGs credit linked stood at 3, 98,974. The cumulative bank loans aggregated Rs.3, 816.32 crores were disbursed during 2006-07, taking the cumulative position to Rs.1543.20 crores for 2, 89,043 SHGs.

INNOVATIONS IN SHG-BANK LINKAGE IN TAMIL NADU

NABARD extends 100% refinance assistance to banks against the financial assistance provided by them to SHGs. In Tamil Nadu, the amount of refinance availed by banks during 2006-07 was of the order of Rs 385.82 crores. NABARD continues to extend financial support to NGOs, Regional Rural Banks, District Cooperative Banks, Farmers Clubs and Individual Rural Volunteers for the promotion and nurturing of SHGs. As part of the innovative strategy to ensure sustainability of SHGs by enhancing the income of the members of the SHGs, NABARD has since introduced grant assistance to NGOs for imparting training on micro enterprises known as Micro Enterprise Development Programme (MEDPs). On a pilot basis, NABARD has provided a marketing platform for SHGs by sponsoring an exhibition of SHG products at Chennai.

Under the Pilot project on SHG-Post Office Linkage, NABARD has been utilizing the services of the trained postal staff in ensuring the savings and credit linkage of SHGs with the Post office as a measure of reaching out to unreached poor. Department of Post is charging a simple interest rate of 9% per annum on the loan amount given to SHGs with no loan processing fees. This project is being implemented in 5 districts namely Pudukottai, Sivaganga, Thanjavur, Thiruvannamalai and Thiruvarur. NABARD also provides Revolving Fund Assistance to MFIs and NGOs for on-lending to SHGs in selected pockets where bank linkage is poor.

With the object of providing assistance to the Tenant Farmers, a separate scheme has been initiated by forming Joint Liability Groups. NABARD also provides equity support to MFIs besides extending support to SHG Federations. NABARD has initiated a Pilot Project for promotion of micro enterprises by members of matured SHGs in 9 districts in the country which included Madurai district in Tamil Nadu.

CONCLUSION

There is a large number of NGOs engaged in model I of SHG-Bank Linkage Programme. It is difficult for the RBI to regulate and supervise these NGOs due to small size and large number. SHG-Bank Linkage Programme should give due weightage for training the poor with the necessary skills to become efficient money managers and successful entrepreneurs. At the mass level awareness should be given about the schemes. It is necessary to shift the focus from the quantity of credit to the quality of credit. It is also necessary to supervise the utilisation of the credit.

SHG-Bank Linkage Programme only focuses on providing financial services to the poor but it should also focus on people's basic needs such as housing, good health, education, social reforms etc. It is also needed to bring an institutional reform in the micro finance strategy of Indian banks as the Grameen Bank did with the introduction of Grameen II.

REFERENCES

Subrahmanya Sarma, Y.V.S. (2008), 'The Micro Finance in India- A Study of SHGs', *Readers Shelf,* Vol. 4, Issue No. 8 J.V. Publishing House, Jodhpour: 3-4.

Banumathi, V.K., (2008), 'Micro Finance in India - An Itinerary to Reach Rural Poor', *Readers Shelf,* Vol. 4, Issue No. 8 J.V. Publishing House, Jodhpur, 1.

Mohammad Abdul Gaffar (2008), 'Micro Credit: A Tool for Poverty Allivation', *Southern Economist,* Vol. 46, No. 23&24, Bangalore, 25-26.

Geeta Manmohan, Monika Tushir and Sumita Chadha (2008), 'Rural Banking and Micro Finance', *Southern Economist,* Vol. 47, No. 2, Bangalore, 9-12.

Madhura Swaminathan (2007), 'The Micro Credit Alternative?', *Economic and Political Weekly,* Vol. XLII, No. 13, Mumbai, 1171-1175.

Niels Hermes and Robert Lensink (2007), 'Impact of Micro Finance: A Critical Survey', *Economic and Political Weekly,* Vol. XLII, No. 6, Mumbai, 462-465.

Satish, P. (2008), 'Misplaced Critique of Micro Finance Regulation Bill', *Economic and Political Weekly,* Vol. XLIII, No. 3, Mumbai 77-79.

Debnarayan Sankar, Indian, (2008), 'Micro Finance: Lessons From Bangladesh', *Economic and Political Weekly,* Vol. XLIII, No. 1, Mumbai, 18-20.

Annual Reports of NABARD, From 2002 To 2008, Mumbai.

14

DIVERGENCE OF LAND REFORMS IN INDIA

P. ANBALAGAN

INTRODUCTION

Land is one of the important four factors of production; agriculture production cannot take place without land. The pattern of ownership of land plays a crucial role in determining the agriculture production, particularly in developing economy. India is an agricultural country in which the prime source of livelihood for a vast majority of people living in rural and tribal areas; land continues to be the pivotal property in terms of both income and employment.

Land reform was one of the parts during the freedom struggle in India. A large number of peasants and landless agricultural labourers were participated in the Civil Disobedience Movement and Non-Cooperation Movement. As a result, in the post- independence era the land reform programme was initiated on the recommendation of Kumarappa Committee. The Five Year Plans incorporated the land reform as one of the important agrarian reforms in India. The main thrust of the Government to include this programme in the Five Year Plans is to directly reduce the intensity of rural poverty and increase agriculture production as well as productivity. Hence, this study has focused to examine land reform programmes and its impact on rural community in India in general. The particular objective this presentation of the paper is to examine the landlessness, poverty, employment and agriculture growth in the state-wise in India. The organization of the paper is as follows. Section I deals with introduction of the study. Section II discussed various available literatures on land reform programme in India. Historical background of the land reform programme discussed in the section III. Evaluation of land reform programme with poverty, unemployment and agricultural growth rate in the IV section. Final section deals with conclusion and summary.

SECTION – II

SURVEY OF LITERATURE

In India, there are numerous case studies on land reforms, of which a few attempts are discussing in this study. Bandyopadhyay's (2008) analyses brought out the historical development of land reform programmes in India. It is alarming that the Naxalism in many parts of the country causes the failure of land reform system. Hence, the author suggests that the transfer of land resources, empowered many powerless persons in rural India is the immediate requirement. Vikas Rawal's (2008) article examines the unequal distribution of agricultural land state-wise in India. This study employed Gini co-efficient, which reveals that inequality of land holding has increased from 0.73 in 1992 to 0.76 in 2003-04. The author also estimated that over 40 per cent of rural households are landless. The study concludes that India have a large potential for redistribution of land in many states. Tim Hanstad et al's (2008) article summarized the efforts taken by the Government of India to implement various land reform programmes. The author highlighted that 12.4 million tenants had benefited of ownership right under the tenancy reform in 2002. It also discussed the wasteland distribution to the rural landless poor. The author concludes that the land reform legislation is a slow progress and link between the rural poverty and landlessness are there in India. Sudha Pai's (2007) study argued that due acquisition of land for various projects like industry, mining, dams, construction of road or railway eviction of rural people has goes up and as a result, landlessness has increased. Mainly people belonging to dalits and tribals are vulnerable groups. Walter Rernandes estimated, between 1951 and 2005 about 55 million persons were forcefully evicted through land acquisition process in India and tribal population constitute 40 percent.

A state level land reform study was conducted by Roy (2001) who examined the role of State Government in the 'agrarian reforms' in Arunachal Pradesh. The empirical result shows that there is high degree of inequalities in distribution of income, assets, land and human capital. The author suggests that removal of landlessness can reduce the inequalities. Timothy Besley (1998) examines the impact of land reform on poverty in India. This paper evolved 16 major Indian state's land reform programmes between 1958 and 1992 and employed regression model for empirical analysis. The result reveals that there is a strong association between poverty reduction and two kinds of land reform legislations viz., tenancy reform and abolition of intermediaries. The result implies that a reduction of All-India poverty gap of 1 per cent can be explained by land reform. This article clearly observed that agriculture can play a significant role on reducing rural poverty. The foregoing review shows that the impact of land reform is multi-dimensional aspect in the economic sense.

SECTION – III

LAND REFORMS IN INDIA

The single most important problem in the developing countries is poverty, resulting from unequal access and use of resources. Though many programmes were introduced in order to reduce the intensity of poverty in the Indian context, land reform programme plays a unique role. The efforts of land distribution to rural landless mass have a positive association with economic growth (Hoff and Lyon, 1995). In the ancient India a complex set of land relations involving private ownership, royal administration and communal rule of villages was is vogue. However, the overlordship of these private lands belonged to the king or the supreme ruler. The king or his intermediary claimed a part of the produce of the land.

In the Medieval India, the Muslim rulers engaged the military personnel and paid them with a plot of land for their services. However, the supreme overlordship of land rested upon the rulers. Later the British rulers realized that land is the key factor in the process of Indian economic development and control land in order to stabilise their rule over the sub-continent. Their first effort was to fix the legal owner of the land as a result land revenue was increased. In the post-independence era, a High Power Committee was setup in 1948 under the chairmanship of Pandit Jawaharlal Nehru and the committee recommended the (i) elimination of intermediaries; (ii) land belonging to non-cultivating owners should be taken over by government; (iii) maximum and minimum size of land holding should be fixed. The Congress Agrarian Reform Committee was recommended the (i) abolition of intermediaries; (ii) encouragement of self cultivation and (iii) tenants reform. All these were adopted by the Government and enacted under the planning.

Land reforms comprise of four categories viz., tenancy reform, abolition of intermediaries, ceilings on land holdings and consolidation of land holdings. Among these, first three categories help in 'poverty alleviation'. This programme was enacted by the various Five Year Plans in India (Appu, 1996). In the First Five Year Plan special emphasis was given to abolition of intermediary; enacted the tenancy law and resumption of cultivation based on peasant proprietorship. Second Five Year Plan enabled the small farmers to resume personal cultivation the time constraint was removal in their case. Third Five Year Plan reiterated the policy accepted by the previous two plans and emphasized the necessarily of quick completion of land reform programme. Fourth Five Year Plan reviewed existing land reforms measures and acknowledged many gap between set objective and actual legislation. Fifth Five Year Plan again re-emphasis and speed up implementation of reform policy; the plan gave high priority to preparation and maintenance of land records. Sixth Five

Year Plan critically evaluated the progress of implementation. Problems relating to land ceiling limit and security of tenure persisted which were looked over by the plan. Seventh Plan decided to remove the inefficiencies of prevailing tenancy law.

Eighth Five Year Plan pays more attention on agrarian reforms. The plan proposes to initiate steps to review and reformulate the land legislations act and ensure effective implementation. In the Ninth Plan, it had been pointed out that rural poverty is largely among the landless and the marginal farmers. Hence, access to land remains a key element in the anti-poverty strategy in rural area during the plan period. The Plan proposed detection and redistribution of surplus land, tenancy reforms for recording rights of tenants, consolidation of holdings and prevention of alienation of tribal lands. The Tenth Five Year Plan carries further the reforms in the agricultural sector which were earlier neglected. The draft of Eleventh Five Year Plan mentioned that has revived the issue of land reform for agricultural efficiency and equality, along with some innovative approaches that would work better for the rural poor. This study envisages that all the Five Year Plans paid priority to redistribution of land to the landless peasants in rural area. Though, the land reform measure has one of the objectives in the Five Year Plans, this has to subject to concern with State Governments. In the post-independence era the State Governments has taken special initiative to implements the land reform through laws in India (Annexure - 1).

SECTION – IV

EVALUATION OF LAND REFORMS IN INDIA

In the first round of land reform (1948- 1954), in different states depicts that the main achievement was the abolition of intermediaries and direct contact of the states with 20 million cultivators. The second phase of reform was concerned with imposition of ceiling on agricultural land, predominantly as redistributive measures. Table 1 presents the structure of land holding in India. The marginal and small farmers consist of a lion share with 80.31 per cent of the total land holders in 1995-96, which was 69.67 per cent in 1970-71. The increment is due to loss of the medium and large farmer's share. The percentage of marginal farmers has rapidly increased from 1970-71 to 1995-96, while the small farmer share has come down from 19.05 per cent to 18.73 per cent in the corresponding period. The medium farmers lost their share at a high level when compared with other categories. This seems to be a progress of the land reform programme implemented in India in the past few decades. Figure 1 clearly depicts the comparison of land holding pattern in two different periods i.e. 1970-71 and 1995-96 in India.

Table 1
Share of Landholding Pattern in India

(in per cent)

Category of Farmers	*1970-71*	*1980-81*	*1990-91*	*1995-96*
Marginal	50.62	56.39	58.99	61.58
Small	19.05	18.08	18.97	18.73
Semi-medium	15.15	14.01	13.21	12.34
Medium	11.25	09.08	07.25	06.14
Large	03.93	02.44	01.59	01.21
All groups	100.00	100.00	100.00	100.00

Source: CMIE, (2007), Agriculture, Centre for Monitoring Indian Economy, Mumbai.

Figure 1: Comparison of Category-wise Landholding Pattern in India (in %)

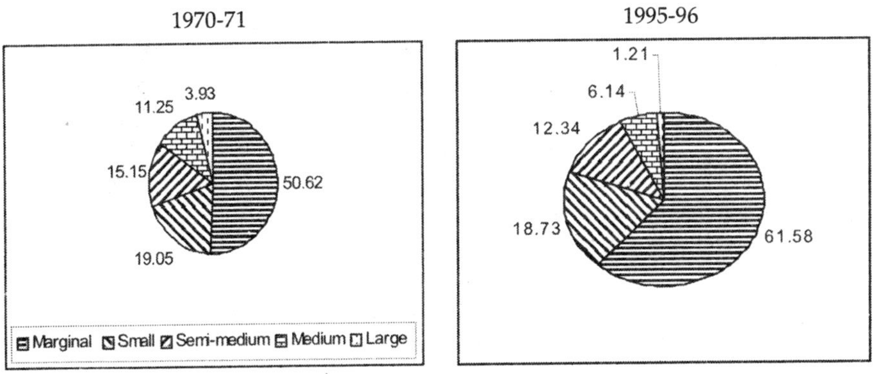

Source: CMIE, (2007), *Agriculture*, Centre for Monitoring Indian Economy, Mumbai.

In the post-independence scenario Indian states passed tenancy reforms laws between 1960s and 1970s however, which is not uniform in nature. The major objective of the act is to assured the tenure security of peasants. The law allowed tenants to acquire ownership or owner like rights to about 4 per cent of India's agricultural land. Hence, the law provides some of exceptions. The central government recommendation to the tenancy reform is to limiting rent range between 20 and 25 per cent of the produce. However, many states followed their own wish. West Bengal succeeded to implement the law due to reasonable fixing the rent. At the end of 2002, 12.4 million tenants on 15.6 million acres of land had benefited. This comprises approximately 8 per cent of all rural households and about 4 per cent of India's cultivated land. The law of tenancy is not much success because the enforcement of the law is very weak in several states in India.

Since independence, Indian states employed several land reform legislations across the country, in which the land ceiling is an important one. Land ceiling varies from state to state because it is states' jurisdiction. Table 2 presents the level of land ceiling state-wise in India. It is observed

Table 2
State-wise Land Ceiling Progress in India

States	Land Ceiling (Acres)	Declared Surplus Land (Acres)	% of Area Taken (%)	% of Area Distribution	Beneficiaries (%)		
					SC	ST	Others
Andhra Pradesh	27.32	800240	78.91	70.87	41.54	15.58	42.88
Bihar	20-60	488257	81.45	62.03	61.70	11.38	26.93
Gujarat	17-132	231172	68.76	57.65	44.38	39.75	15.87
Karanataka	27	280779	59.11	42.29	60.33	03.10	36.57
Kerala	15-37.5	137692	68.85	46.69	42.85	05.12	52.03
Madhya Pradesh	25-50	338555	88.30	54.71	29.85	37.43	32.73
Maharashtra	18-126	729644	90.93	76.05	29.84	20.78	49.38
Orissa	25	176569	93.57	87.11	33.93	37.25	28.82
Pubjab	50	132594	79.09	77.84	39.95	–	60.05
Rajasthan	30	600987	92.88	75.13	41.90	01.25	56.85
Tamil Nadu	30	197311	89.44	83.29	44.16	00.14	55.71
Uttar Pradesh	40	555350	93.84	69.13	69.33	00.23	30.43
West Bengal	02	1270965	94.57	75.66	37.22	19.51	43.27
All India	–	7884132	83.68	65.85	36.20	14.08	49.71

Source: Gyaneshwar Ojha, *Land Problems and Land Reforms*, Sultan Chand & Sons, New Delhi; and Rural Development Statistics (1999), National Institute of Rural Development, Hyderabad.

that there is no uniformity among the states in fixing the upper limit of land ceiling. The upper limit of the ceiling is higher in Gujarat and Maharashtra. By the end of 2002, State governments had declared 7.4 million acres of land as exceeding the ceilings. Of that, the state governments had taken possession of 6.5 million acres and distributed 5.4 million to a total of 5.6 million households. The total amounts to approximately 1.4 per cent of India's agricultural land (Government of India, 2002-03). West Bengal, Assam and Jammu and Kashmir are the predominant states to significantly implement the land ceiling Act.

Estimation of surplus land was remarkably high in West Bengal, and the subsequent rank was occupied by Andhra Pradesh and Maharashtra. In many states are significant proportion of surplus land has not been taken under possession. In Karnataka, only 59 per cent of the surplus area has come under possession. West Bengal, Uttar Pradesh, Orissa, Rajasthan and Maharashtra accounted more than 90 per cent of area. In almost all the states considerable part of land which has been taken under possession is not distributed. In Karnataka only 42 per cent of area declared surplus has been distributed, in Kerala covered 47 per cent. Maharashtra, Punjab, West Bengal and Rajasthan are more than 75 per cent of area declared surplus has been distributed. Though, the national guideline suggests that 50 per cent of the land to be distributed though land reform measures should be made available to Schedule Caste (SC) and Schedule Tribes (ST) beneficiaries, the discrimination pattern in states like Tamil Nadu,, Punjab, Maharashtra, Rajasthan and Kerala reveals a bias in favour of the non-scheduled groups. Bihar, Karnataka and Uttar Pradesh are favour for the SC beneficiaries. Madhya Pradesh and Maharashtra has less favour for the SCs to distribute the surplus land. Orissa and Madhya Pradesh, ST beneficiaries are high with about 37 per cent. At All India level, the distribution land norms were followed and favour to the SC and ST population. (Mohanty, 2001). Indian states have not seriously implemented the land ceiling policy hence, some bottlenecks are witnessed in implementing the land ceiling programme such as lack of political will and less effort has taken by the State Governments. Many state's land ceilings have not led to a significant distribution of land, those ceiling may be serving a useful role in preventing a further excessive concentration of land and in providing appropriate incentives for some large landowners to sell land to small farmers and or diversify into the non-agricultural sector (Tim Hanstad et al, 2008).

LAND REFORMS AND ECONOMIC DEVELOPMENT

As the land reform has one of the major cause for production and productivity of agriculture, Table 3 shows the economic and agriculture development in India for the last six decades.

Table 3
Average Gross Domestic Product Growth Rate of Agriculture in India

(in %)

Description	*Total Economy*	*Agriculture and Allied*
Pre-Green revolution 1951-52 to 1967-68	3.69	2.54
Green revolution period 1968-69 to 1980-81	3.52	2.44
Period between 1981-82 and 1990-91	5.52	2.50
Early reform period 1991-92 and 1996-97	5.69	3.66
Ninth Five Year Plan 1997-98 to 2001-02	5.52	2.50
Tenth Five Year Plan 2002-03 to 2006-07	7.77	2.47

Source: Planning Commission, Eleventh Five Year Plan 2007-2012, Government of India.

The aggregate economic growth accelerated since mid of 1980s due to implementation of liberalization policy. The average growth rate of economy was registered 5.69 per cent in the early period of the liberalization which has considerably increased in the Tenth Five Year Plan with 7.7 per cent. When compared to the overall economic growth with agriculture performance the later has registered less significant. Agriculture sector percentage of contribution to the GDP has drastically comedown since post-independence era in India due to environmental factors, structural transformation sectoral transformation and political interference. Unequal distribution of wealth and income are the major cause for this poor performance, particularly SC, ST and OBCs are deprived their rights to claim land ownership.

National Sample Survey Organisation (NSSO) also states that higher level of landlessness was little over 40 per cent in terms of operational holdings (only agricultural land). The data set also shows that at All India level marginal and small land owners constituted 90.40 per cent of the total number of owners and owned only 43.43 per cent of land whereas the medium and large farmers constituted only 9.60 per cent of landowners owned 56.21 per cent of land. This is very clear that the distribution of wealth among the farmers is not significant. The main reason is that the law is in favour of land distribution, which is also deliberately provides loopholes to enable big land owners to evade the law and thus, land ceiling act is not really effective tool in many parts of Indian subcontinent.

Table 4 shows the extent of landlessness across different states by two different measures of landlessness i.e. those who do not own any land either homestead or otherwise and the second category belongs to those who do not have any land other than homestead. Households that do not have homestead are among the lowest in Kerala. All the southern states are significant level of homestead except Karnataka. It may be noted that a large number of households in Kerala were provided with homestead lands as a part of land reforms. Table 4 also reveals that Maharashtra accounted top at All India level with 17.66 per cent of households do not have any land followed by Tamil Nadu with 16.55 per cent. Uttar Pradesh registered lowest households do not have any kind of land. The estimation show that eight Indian states including the major states Maharashtra, Tamil Nadu, Andhra Pradesh, Madhya Pradesh and Karnataka percentage of do not have any kind of land is higher than the national average.

Figure 2 reveals the state-wise landlessness in India. Several researchers have shown that the many of these households use homesteads for cultivation of commercial crops.

Poverty is an important obstacle for slow growth of an economy. Table 4 reveals that the state-wise rural poverty in India. World-wide, many nations witnessed less urban poverty than rural poverty. In India, poverty is not uniform across the states or regions. Incidence of poverty is lower in south, west and north-west parts of India. Orissa recorded highest incidence of poverty in the rural, followed by Jharkhand and Bihar. Three states namely Maharashtra, Tamil Nadu and Uttaranchal greatly succeeded in reducing the rural poverty in 2004-05. The incidence of rural poverty in Punjab and Gujarat was lower in 1983 but it was revitalized in the year 2004-05 i.e. urban poverty is higher in percentage. Between 1983 and 2004-05, the degree of rural poverty reduction is higher in West Bengal with 35.1 per cent, followed by Tamil Nadu 32.1 per cent and Kerala 26.4 per cent. At All-India level, rural poverty has come down from 46.5 per cent in 1983 to 28.7 per cent in 2004-05. Equal distribution

Table 4

State-wise Landless Pattern, Rural Poverty, Unemployment and Agriculture Growth in India

(in per cent)

States	*Do Not Own Any Land*	*Rank*	*Do Not Own Any Land Other than Homestead*	*Rural Poverty (2004-2005)*	*Rank*	*Unemployment (2004-2005)*	*Agriculture Growth Rate (1995-96 - 2004-05)*
Andhra Pradesh	14.33	4	53.19	10.8	17	10.9	2.69
Assam	8.05	11	40.30	21.7	10	6.5	0.95
Jharkhand	4.80	15.5	39.25	42.9	2	NA	NA
Bihar	7.60	13	38.8	42.2	3	6.8	3.51
Gujarat	13.60	6	44.11	19.4	12	4.1	0.48
Haryana	9.21	10	49.49	13.6	16	6.2	1.98
HimachalPradesh	15.00	3	22.68	10.9	15	NA	NA
Karnataka	14.09	5	40.47	20.0	11	6.7	0.03
Kerala	4.80	15.5	68.36	13.2	14	25.6	-3.54
Chhattisgarh	12.09	7	27.31	42.0	4	NA	NA
Madhya Pradesh	12.05	8	31.81	35.8	5	5.6	-0.23
Maharashtra	17.66	1	44.78	30.0	7	9.3	0.10
Orissa	9.56	9	38.48	46.9	1	10.2	0.11
Pubjab	4.57	17	56.89	10.0	18	9.7	2.16
Rajasthan	5.56	14	19.95	19.0	13	4.4	0.30
Tamil Nadu	16.55	2	64.52	22.7	9	15.1	-1.36
Uttar Pradesh	3.82	18	26.20	33.9	6	3.7	1.87
West Bengal	6.15	12	46.52	28.5	8	11.2	2.67
All India	10.04	–	41.63	28.7	–	8.2	1.85

Note: Landless data related to the year 2003-04 and poverty related to the year 2004-05

Source: National Sample Survey Organization, 59th round for landholding pattern; poverty 61st round, unemployment and agriculture growth from Planning Commission, Eleventh Five Year Plan 2007- 2012, Government of India.

Figure 2: State-wise Landlessness in India (2003-04)

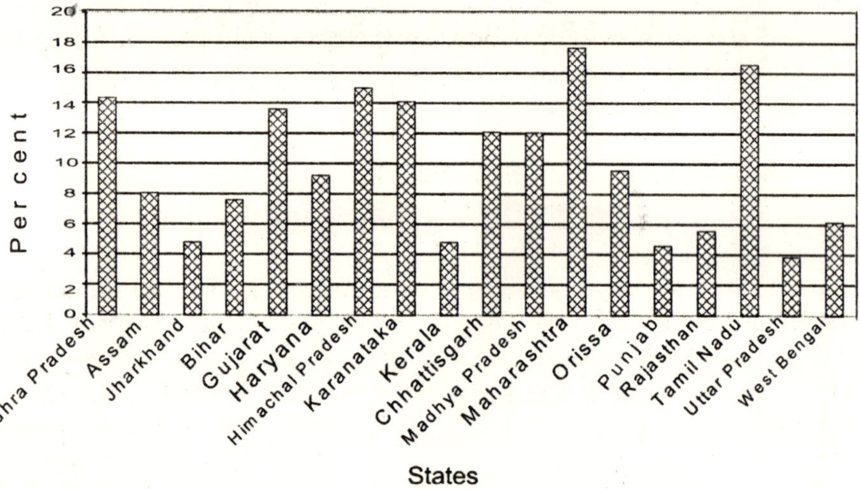

of land and agriculture growth is the main factor to generate more employment in the rural in turn which has reduces the poverty intensity. Hence, in this study it is clear that Kerala is the top state in unemployment followed by Tamil Nadu. The rate of unemployment is the lowest in Uttar Pradesh at 3.7 per cent.

EMPIRICAL ANALYSIS

Reduction of landlessness seems to increase agriculture production and productivity in that process this can generate income which in turn can reduce the rural poverty. This study has employed Spearman's rank correlation to test the relationship between four variables i.e. Landlessness (LN), Rural Poverty (RP), Agriculture Growth (AG) and Unemployment (UN).

Table 5
Empirical result of Landlessness with Related Variables

Variables	*Rank Correlation*
LN to RP	0.090
LN to UN	0.044
LN to AG	0.767

Source: Same in Table 4, values are computed.

The empirical results of Spearman's rank correlation show that landlessness is positively associated with rural poverty, unemployment and agricultural growth rate however, agriculture growth is significantly and positively associated than the other two variables. Poverty and unemployment are major obstacles for the nation. Landlessness is considered as one of the evil of the society therefore, existing bottlenecks in the land reform programme should be removed in order to improve the overall socioeconomic development of rural community. The loopholes in the laws have to be arrested and a vigorous implementation of existing law is an immediate need for the society.

SECTION – V

CONCLUSION

Equal distribution of wealth has to be an important step to reduce the intensity of poverty in India. The Union and State Governments in India have taken a robust measure to reduce the gap between the rich and poor through the land reforms, which is especially benefiting the rural community. Even sixty years after independence a chunk of India's peasants still struggling for claiming land ownership rights. This study very clearly shows that the rural poverty is high compared with the urban because of the landless peasants are in a large volume. In order to benefit the landless peasant, government has to enact a common policy measure across the country. Government machinery has failed to acquire all surplus land from the landlords and further the distribution of surplus land to the landless peasant is not strictly followed. The government should take necessary step to provide the power for powerless person in rural community. All the peasant should be ensured of equal land share, which will pave the way for enjoying their social, economical and political privileges in the global village.

REFERENCES

Appu, P.S. (1996), *Land Reforms in India: A Survey of Policy Legislation and Implementation*, Vikas, New Delhi.

Balagopal, K. (2007), Ceiling Surpluses and Public lands, *Economic and Political Weekly*, No. XLII, No. 38, September 22, 2007, pp. 3829-3832.

Bandyopadhyay, D. (2008), Does Land Still Matter?, *Economic and Political Weekly*, No. XLIII, No. 10, March 8-14, 2008, pp. 37-42.

CMIE, (2007), *Agriculture*, Centre for Monitoring Indian Economy, Mumbai.

Government of India, (2002-03), *Annual Report 2002-03*, Ministry of Rural Development, Government of India.

Government of India (2006), *Agricultural Statistics at a Glance*, Ministry of Agriculture (*http://agricoop.nic.in*)

Government of India (2008), *Eleventh Five Year Plan 2007-2012*, Planning Commission Government of India.

Hoff, Karla and Andrew B. Lyon, (1995), Non-leaky Buckets: Optimal Redistributive Taxationand Agency Costs, *Journal of Public Economics*, 58, 365-390.

Khusro, A.M. (1973), *Economic of Land Reform and Farm Size in India,* Macmillian India, Madras.

Mohanty, B.B (2001), Land Distribution among Scheduled Caste and Tribes, *Economic and Political Weekly,* October 6 2001.

Roy, N. C. (2001), *Land Reform in Arunachal Pradesh,* Classical Pulishing Company, New Delhi.

Russell King (1997), *Land Reform – A World Survey,* G. Bell & Sons Ltd., London.

Tim Hanstad, T. Haque, Robin Nielsen, (2008), Improving Land Access for India's Rural Poor, *Economic and Political Weekly,* March 8, 2008.

Rural Development Statistics (199), National Institute of Rural Development, Hyderabad.

Sharma, H.R. (1994), Landholdings in Rural India, 1953-54 to 1981-82: Implications of Land Reforms, *Economic and Political Weakly,* September 24.

Sudha Pai (2007), Janadesh (2007), The Land Question,, *Economic and Political Weekly,* November 17, 2007.

Timothy Besley and Robin Burgess, (1998), *Land Reform, Poverty Reduction and Growth: Evidence from India,* Landon School of Economics, London.

Vikas Rawal (2008), Ownership Holdings of Land in Rural India: Putting the Record Straight, *Economic and Political Weekly,* March 8.

ANEXURE
IMPORTANT EVENTS IN LAND REFORMS IN THE INDIA STATES

State	*Land Reforms Laws*
Andhra Pradesh	Tenancy and Agricultural Land Act 1950; Hyderabad Abolition of Cash Grants Act 1952; Inams Abolition Act 1954; Hyderabad Jagidars Act 1955; Inam Act, Tenancy Act 1956; Inams Abolition Act 1957
Assam	Zamindari Act 1951; Lushai Hill District Act 1954; Fixation of Ceiling on Land Holding Act 1956; Consolidation of Holding Act 1960; Tenancy Act 1971.
Karnataka	Mysore Inam Abolition Act 1954; Mysore Inams Abolition Act 1955; Land Reforms Act 1961; Land Reforms Act 1974.
Kerala	Agrarian Relations Act 1960; Land Reforms Act 1963; Land Reforms Act 1969; Agricultural Workers Act 1974.
Madhya Pradesh	Abolition of Proprietary Right Act 1950; Zamindari Abolition Act 1951; Abolition of Jagir Act 1951; Land Reform Act 1959; Ceiling on agricultural Holdins Acts 1960.
Bihar	Land Reforms Act 1950; Homestead Tenancy Act 1957; Land Reforms Act 1961; Land Ceiling Act 1961; Act 12 1973; Act 55 1976; Tenancy Act 1982.
Gujarat	Bombay Tenancy and Agricultural Lands Act 1948; Agricultural Lands Ceiling Act 1960; Devasthan Inam Abolition Act 1969; Amending Act 1973.
Haryana	Punjab Security of Land Tenures Act 1953; Pepus Tenancy and Agricultural Land Act 1955.
Jammu & Kashmir	Agrarian Reforms Act 1962, 1976
Maharashtra	Hyderabad Tenancy and Agricultural Lands Act 1950; Bombay Tenancy and Agricultural Land Act 1958; Agricultural Land Act 1961.
Orissa	Estate Abolition Act 1951; Land Reforms Act 1972; Land Reforms Act 1960
Punjab	Punjab Security of Land Tenure Act 1953; Pepsu Tenancy and Agricultural Land Act 1955; Land Reforms Act 1972.

(*Annexure Continued*)

State	*Land Reforms Laws*
Rajasthan	Land Reforms and Jagir Act1952;Bombay Merged Act1953;Abolition of Intermediaries and Land Reforms Act 1955; Tenancy Act1955;Zamindari Act 1959
Tamil Nadu	Estates Act 1948; Tenants Act 1952; Tenants Protection Act 1955; Cultivating Tenants Act 1956; ; Land Reforms Act.1961; Tenancy Right Act 1961; Right Act 1969; rural Artisan Act 1976.
Uttar Pradesh	Zamindari Abolition and Land Reforms Act 1950; Consolidation of Holdings Act 1953; Imposition of Ceilings on Landholdings Act 1960.
West Bengal	Bargadars Act 1950; Estates Acquisition Act 1953; Land Reforms Act 1955; Homestead Land Act 1972; Acquisition of Homestead land for Agri.labours, Artisans and Fisherman Act 1975; Land Reforms Act 1977; Land Reforms Act 1981; Land Reforms Act 1986; Land Reforms Act 1980.